# OPTIMIZE
## YOUR 401(k)

# OPTIMIZE YOUR 401(k)

## SEIZE OPPORTUNITIES, AVOID PITFALLS, BUILD WEALTH, → AND MAKE MILLION$

WILLIAM A. BADER, JD, CPA

Published by What Matters in Retirement Press, Short Hills, NJ

**GIRL FRIDAY**
PRODUCTIONS

Edited and designed by Girl Friday Productions
www.girlfridayproductions.com

Cover design: Brad Foltz
Project management: Sara Spees Addicott
Editorial production: Katherine Richards
Image credits: cover Shutterstock/afry_harvy

ISBN (paperback): 979-8-218-57803-9
ISBN (ebook): 979-8-218-58415-3

Library of Congress Control Number: 2025902129

First edition

*To my wife, Cheryl, whose unwavering support, love, and encouragement have been my greatest strength during the writing of this book and throughout our marriage. And to my children, Alison and Jeremy, whose love has inspired me every step of the way—this book is as much yours as it is mine.*

# CONTENTS

## PART III: PROBLEMS

## PART IV: TALES AND CONCLUSION

# INTRODUCTION

The scent of fresh mozzarella and homemade pasta whet my appetite while I enjoyed a glass of Chardonnay with my friend Barry. He expressed concern about his father-in-law, Chris, who had recently retired at age sixty-nine and was worried about his pension. Barry explained that Chris's pension plan had delayed the $5,000 monthly payment for five months, for a total holdback of $25,000. These shortfalls were bad enough, but as Barry and I spoke further, it became clear that this was more than just a $25,000 problem—it was exponentially larger. Chris had never received a required notice from the plan stating his eligibility to retire and start collecting his pension at age sixty-five. Since this notice was not provided, Chris was entitled to his $5,000 monthly payments *starting at age sixty-five*, as if he had retired then. That meant the plan owed him forty-eight monthly payments at $5,000 each for a grand total of $240,000—plus interest!

This common error often goes unnoticed. I prepared a letter to the plan administrator, and Chris was pleasantly surprised with a $240,000 check in corrective pension payments. He received interest on top of that. This was no small feat, considering that the employer in question was one of the largest companies in the world. The amount was life-changing for Chris.

Throughout my career, I have uncovered numerous mistakes by plan administrators that have significantly reduced benefits for employees. In this book, I call these *problems*. But I have also seen many employees not use their plans optimally. For example, some invest too conservatively for their age or do not contribute enough to get the full match. I see these as missed opportunities—chances that, if acted upon, can improve one's financial future. These experiences opened my eyes to the crucial importance of maximizing retirement benefits, and they inspired me to share my knowledge. I hope to help readers take control of their financial future and have the flexibility to live on their terms.

Financial planning is like traveling on a long journey; many opportunities and potential problems exist, and you are the chief executive officer (CEO) of your financial strategy. The CEO oversees a company's business by establishing goals, confirming implementation of those goals, and continually reviewing performance. Similarly, in our lives, we should strive to be the CEOs of our financial future by establishing and revising our personal goals, taking steps to achieve them, and monitoring their progress. As you read this book, you will learn to manage your 401(k) or other financial retirement affairs with the skill of a CEO. This process does not require side gigs, crypto investments, or complex unintelligible strategies. Ignore these get-rich-quick schemes and focus on the important issues. What your journey *does* require is patience, time, and persistence.

Retirement can be a beautiful chapter of life, and I hope this book will help you achieve just that. Grab your glass of wine or favorite drink and join me on this journey.

## THE RETIREMENT CRISIS

Sitting on a beach or playing golf in Florida daily, without stress or anxiety, might seem like a far-off dream. Unfortunately, for more than 100 million Americans, that dream may never come true. The National Institute on Retirement Security (NIRS), a nonprofit research and education organization that provides data and insights on retirement security to policymakers, conducted a study in 2018 and found that more than 59% of people who are able to work—more than 100 million people—do not own any retirement assets in a 401(k) plan, individual retirement account (IRA), or pension.[1]

According to some experts, there is a retirement crisis in America right now, and it will not go away anytime soon. The same NIRS study drives this home with additional sobering statistics:[2]

- The median retirement account balance among all employed people, including those without retirement accounts, is $0.00. In other words, the typical working American has *no* retirement savings.
- 68% of people aged fifty-five to sixty-four have retirement savings of less than one year's income, significantly less than what they will need to maintain their lifestyle once they stop working.
- A typical employed American must replace 85% of pre-retirement income when they retire. About 35% of this will come from Social Security (which some say may not be paid by the government at some point in the future due to insufficient funding). The remaining 50% must come from other sources of income, such as a 401(k) plan, IRA, or other forms of wealth accumulation.

According to a 2024 survey, 79% of Americans believe there is a retirement crisis, up from 67% in 2020.[3] In addition, a 2023 study found that 50% of families won't be able to retire and afford their pre-retirement lifestyle.[4]

Setting aside funds for your financial future is often challenging and overwhelming for almost everyone because of the current financial pressures to pay for essentials like rent and food. You're not the only one going through this. This book is here to help you get the most out of your hard work, providing useful tools and tips, to prepare yourself for the future. Starting early with consistent contributions, for example, will lead to significant savings, potentially even millions of dollars. Teachers, coaches, small business owners, and others have been able to do this by slowly saving and investing over decades, which means you can do this too. It isn't easy, but it can be done.

## WHAT YOU CAN EXPECT FROM THIS BOOK

The following chapters provide extensive information to help you optimize your retirement benefits. They cover common issues and opportunities in retirement planning, concentrating mostly on 401(k) plans. They contain actionable advice and real-life examples to clarify important points. Each chapter also includes summary points.

While the book is mostly about 401(k) plans, it recognizes that many people today are self-employed or run small businesses and may wish to establish and participate in retirement plans even though a 401(k) isn't available to them. Additionally, 401(k) participants may also be eligible for an IRA in certain circumstances. Therefore, a separate chapter covers these opportunities, including traditional and Roth IRAs and other plans for small business owners. The goal is to provide tailored advice to easily help the reader quickly determine which issues are relevant and take quick action.

*Part I: Begin to Win, the Basics Within:* This section introduces important financial concepts in an easy-to-understand way. Starting here will help you understand the reasoning behind the recommendations in later chapters and provide tools for using them. We begin with 401(k) basics, such as matching contributions and the difference between Roth and traditional contributions. Next, basic investing concepts such as stocks, bonds, and mutual funds are covered.

You will discover the most important action you can take with your money, how much to save for a secure retirement, and tools to help with these tasks. We will also discuss challenging financial topics, like credit card debt, which makes saving money difficult. Reviewing and understanding this fundamental information will help you evaluate the material that follows and make the best choices for your situation.

*Part II: Opportunities:* This section discusses and analyzes eleven important opportunities to consider and use strategically. They include investing effectively, maximizing matching contributions, and evaluating Roth contributions. This part also covers a few items that may seem like opportunities on the surface but are traps to avoid. Like a wolf in sheep's clothing, these fake opportunities can be hard to recognize, but you'll learn what to watch for.

*Part III: Problems:* This section covers eight major problems that can harm your retirement savings, such as improperly being excluded from participating in your 401(k) plan, miscalculated matching contributions, and other common administrative errors. It will also review practical ideas to help you recover your legally earned benefits should you encounter these problems.

*Part IV: Tales and Conclusion:* It's always helpful to hear how other people have found success. In this section, you'll find real-life examples of people who live within their means, save diligently, and are on their way to a safe financial future—and those who did not always make the right choices. We will close with some inspiring words to get you on your way.

*Glossary and Appendixes:* Concepts surrounding retirement planning involve a lot of terms that may be unfamiliar to readers, so a glossary of key terms is included for easy reference. This section also includes several appendixes that support the advice and conclusions presented in this book and endnotes.

## MY BACKGROUND

I was a retirement consultant and worldwide partner at Mercer, one of the largest global retirement consulting firms, where I spent over twenty-five years. In this role, I reviewed hundreds of 401(k), profit-sharing, pension, and other retirement plans sponsored by various companies. These reviews often uncovered issues with plan administration that adversely affected participant account values. During my career, I have also seen common errors that employees make, often resulting in significant retirement savings losses. Before joining Mercer, I practiced 401(k), pension, and tax law at several well-respected law firms, including Fried Frank. In addition to being an attorney, I am also a CPA. I received my undergraduate degree at the Wharton School of Business and my law degree at Hofstra Law School.

## VISUALIZE YOUR RETIREMENT

Before you begin reading, please take a moment to think about what retirement looks like to you. Imagine retiring early at fifty, sleeping peacefully on a sunny beach, enjoying a round of golf, tending to an organic farm, traveling the world, or even working part-time in a field you care deeply about. Savings accumulated by then will help provide the flexibility to pursue any vision if you follow the ideas in the following pages.

# AUTHOR'S NOTE

This book is designed to provide general information and guidance on 401(k) plans and investing based on my personal experiences, knowledge, and research at the time of publication. The information in this book reflects laws, regulations, and industry practices as of the publication date. Future changes in the laws, regulations, and industry practices may alter the applicability or accuracy of the material presented.

This book is for educational purposes only and is not intended to provide specific investment, legal, or tax advice. In addition, the book is not a substitute for personalized financial advice. Investment strategies and retirement planning are highly situational, and what works for one person may not work for another.

All investments carry inherent risks, including fluctuations in value due to market conditions. While this book discusses historical market performance, trends, and investment strategies, past performance does not guarantee future results. Investing involves risk, including the potential loss of principal. Readers should evaluate their risk tolerance and financial goals when implementing any strategy discussed in this book.

References to specific financial products, services, or companies are included for illustrative purposes and do not constitute endorsements or recommendations.

Readers should consult a qualified financial advisor, tax professional, or legal expert before making significant financial decisions.

I have included endnotes with citations to materials that provide additional insights and context to assist with your due diligence. These resources can help you deepen your understanding of the topics discussed and evaluate how they might apply to your unique financial situation.

# PART I

Begin to Win,
the Basics Within

# CHAPTER 1

## Common Features of Retirement Plans

This chapter provides important background on the types of retirement plans offered in the private sector (excluding government-run plans) and their key features. This general overview will facilitate understanding the material in later chapters, which will go into much more detail.

Our focus here is primarily on *defined contribution plans*. In these plans, contributions are made to the participant's account by the employee, the employer, or both. Once the contributions are made, the participant decides how to invest these funds. Almost every plan offers a choice of investment options, typically an assortment of mutual funds. In some plans, the employer's company stock is offered as an investment option. The participant bears all the investment-related risk in a defined contribution plan and is not guaranteed a benefit at retirement. Generally, taxes are paid upon distribution, except for Roth accounts.

In *defined benefit plans*, participants are guaranteed a benefit payable as an annuity for their life, normally beginning when they retire. The employer is responsible for setting and managing the funds; distributions are generally taxable. Defined benefit pension plans have been decreasing in popularity in the United States for years.

While plan features may vary significantly, federal law, the Employee Retirement Income Security Act (ERISA), has established minimum standards and procedures for nearly all plans. While your employer is not legally required to offer a plan, it must follow these minimum standards and procedures if it does.

## TYPES OF DEFINED CONTRIBUTION PLANS

The widely offered *traditional 401(k) plan* is a defined contribution plan that provides significant tax advantages for the employer. Its name comes from the Internal Revenue Code section governing these plans. Employees can contribute a portion of their salary to their accounts through payroll withholding, and many employers then match some or all of the employee contributions, although a match is not required. The terms of the match are covered in the plan document, which the employer controls. The employer match is my favorite 401(k) feature because *it's like getting free money.* You will learn to take full advantage of this feature, which can sometimes be tricky. Also, earnings are not taxed while they remain invested in the plan. Employee and employer contributions are subject to limits imposed by the Internal Revenue Code and the plan terms.

*Roth 401(k) plan contributions* are similar to traditional plan contributions, and most employers offer both traditional and Roth. The difference is generally in the way they are taxed. A traditional 401(k) reduces the employee's income taxes in the year contributions are made because the earnings that were withheld and deposited directly into the 401(k) account aren't subject to tax. However, those contributions and earnings are taxed when the money is ultimately distributed from the account to the participant.

Roth contributions, on the other hand, are made with after-tax amounts, meaning that all of the employee's earnings are considered fully taxable, and the taxes on those earnings are deducted from the contributions before they are sent to the Roth 401(k). However, distributions later withdrawn from the account, usually upon retirement, and associated income earned on the contributions over the years are tax-free.

In 2024, the maximum an employee could contribute each year to any 401(k) plan, including Roth and traditional contributions, was $23,000. Most 401(k) plans also include a *catch-up contribution* feature, which allows participants age fifty and over to increase contributions to their 401(k) plans as retirement is rapidly approaching. This feature is a nice "second bite at the apple" when people can most afford it after they've raised their families, settled into their homes, and so on. In 2024, employees could make an additional catch-up contribution each year of $7,500. Therefore, those who are age fifty and over had a total limit of $30,500 annually.

The *profit-sharing plan* is another defined contribution plan. The employer determines the amount contributed, which is often based on compensation (e.g., 5%) and may vary from year to year. Employer contributions and earnings to this type of plan are taxable to the employee in the year they are withdrawn. This is a fantastic benefit you may be fortunate to enjoy—more free money!

Tax shelters are often mentioned in the news or in advertisements as investment vehicles for the wealthy. However, tax shelters are not only for the rich and don't have to involve Swiss bank accounts or other shady schemes. Meet the 401(k) retirement tax shelter for everyone: Tax shelters are *legal* ways for a taxpayer to protect (or shelter) income from taxation.

**401(k) and other plans, such as profit-sharing plans and IRAs, allow you to pay taxes later, when your tax rates may be lower after you've retired, thereby reducing your tax burden and protecting your income.**

## PLAN FEATURES

*Participation:* All plans contain rules for determining eligibility and often exclude certain classes of employees, like hourly or commission based. Employees may be legally excluded as long as several technical rules are met. You should review your plan's *summary plan description* (SPD) to determine its rules and see if you are covered. Even if you are covered, the plan may require you to be at least age twenty-one and have a year of service (typically, no more than five hundred or one thousand hours are required in the year) before participation can start. A plan may not exclude an employee who has reached a maximum age (e.g., sixty).

Many 401(k) plans automatically enroll participants. This means employees do not have to opt in to participate; instead, it allows them to opt out if they choose not to participate. Most employees will take no action and opt into the plan by default, thereby building their retirement funds by doing nothing.

*Vesting:* Vesting means you own the contributions and earnings in your retirement account and cannot forfeit them. In a 401(k) plan, you are always 100% vested in the contributions you make and the earnings on those amounts. But in most defined contribution plans, such as profit-sharing and 401(k) plans, you will likely have to work for several years before becoming fully vested in your company's contributions, including 401(k) matching contributions and related earnings. The vesting schedule is described in the plan document.

A variety of different vesting schedules are commonly used. One involves immediate vesting in company contributions after three years of service. This is known as *cliff vesting* because you aren't vested in any portion before working for three years. Alternatively, a graded vesting schedule may apply, where you become at least 20% vested after two years, 40% after three years, 60% after four years, 80% after five years, and 100% vested after six years. A two-year vesting schedule, in which you are not vested in any portion before working for two years, is sometimes provided in 401(k) plans with automatic enrollment features, where the employer must make a minimum contribution, which becomes fully vested after two years of service.

A plan can always vest company contributions more quickly; the above schedules are the maximum number of years that may be required under applicable law. Hopefully, yours will vest quickly.

Importantly, when you become vested, you own the portion of your benefit that is vested, but you still may not be able to withdraw it from the plan until later. Your plan and applicable law control when you can withdraw your benefits.

*Withdrawing your benefit:* The plan document explains when

a distribution, also known as a *withdrawal*, can be made (e.g., at retirement) and the available distribution options (e.g., lump sum). This information is also contained in the SPD, which explains the plan document in plain English and is far easier to understand. Reading of the SPD should be required for all plan participants! I am half joking, but it *is* an excellent resource to learn about the money you worked so hard for.

You must generally start withdrawing your retirement benefits no later than April 1, following the calendar year you attain age seventy-three (seventy-five starting in 2033, which affects those born in 1960 and later) or the year you retire (if later than those ages). Beyond retirement, there are sometimes other events, such as termination of employment, that may enable you to take a distribution under some plan types (401(k) and profit sharing) but not others (pension plans). 401(k) plans often allow distributions while employed if the participant reaches age fifty-nine and a half or incurs a hardship, and most allow participants to borrow money from their accounts. Profit-sharing plans may allow distributions while the employee still works at the company once they achieve a specified number of years of service.

*Required information:* Depending on the type of retirement plan and when you meet the plan's eligibility requirements, you should receive several documents. These include an SPD, enrollment package, beneficiary designation, and salary deferral election form. The plan must also provide certain written notices, some automatically and others upon request. Online notices are permissible by law if certain requirements are met.

*Filing a claim for benefits:* All plans must have a reasonable procedure for processing a claim for benefits. Your plan's claim procedures are explained in the SPD. If you have a problem regarding your benefits, such as whether the amount is correct, you can file a formal claim under the plan's claim procedure rules.

*Seeking help:* Besides creating rights for plan participants, ERISA imposes duties on people who use their discretion or judgment in operating your plan. These *fiduciaries* have a legal duty to act prudently and in the interests of plan participants and beneficiaries, and they generally include investment managers, trustees, and plan administrators. If you have questions about your plan, the first place to start is with your SPD. If you need additional assistance, you should contact the plan administrator. The SPD should provide information on how to do this. See appendix B for more information.

*Plan mergers and terminations:* If your company merges with another company, your plan will likely change. Common changes include investment options and recordkeeper changes.

If your plan is terminated, all affected participants become fully vested, regardless of the plan's vesting schedule.

## SUMMARY

- Most private-sector retirement plans are defined contribution plans.
- 401(k) and other retirement plans are legal tax shelters that help you defer your taxes and protect your income.
- The SPD describes your plan's participation, vesting, withdrawal, and other important features.

# CHAPTER 2

## Building Your Investment Knowledge Base

Bank accounts can be a safe haven for your savings, but the modest returns will be insufficient for almost everyone. While billionaires may succeed with this approach, most of us require investment options with much higher returns to achieve financial flexibility and a comfortable retirement. This is where 401(k) plans come into play, offering a crucial solution to this financial challenge. They are a popular choice for many, typically offering a diverse range of investment options carefully selected by your company or an external advisor. This variety allows you to tailor your investments to align with your financial goals, and this chapter will introduce you to some of the most popular options and key topics. Important investing concepts include risk mitigation, asset allocation, diversification, domestic stocks, international stocks, bonds, and index investing.

### THE US STOCK MARKET

When you buy a share of stock, you receive and own a small piece of a company. This type of investment is often called *equity* because equity means ownership. If the company does well, it is rewarded, and so are you as an investor or owner in the form of *returns*. On the contrary, if your investment does poorly, the value of your stock diminishes, and you can lose part or all of it. Stock returns measure the gain or loss from a stock investment over a specified period. These returns include increases in the stock price, known as *capital gains*, and *dividends*, which are a distribution of profits to the investor. For example, if I purchase a share of stock for $40, sell it in a year for $60, and receive a $2 dividend during the same year, the capital gain is $20 ($60 – $40). But in this case, my *annual return* is 55%—the capital gain plus the dividend divided by the initial investment ($22 ÷ $40).

**Investing in stocks has historically offered high returns and outperformed other investments, such as bonds or savings accounts, over long periods. It has been one of the greatest wealth-generation opportunities over the long term and has always increased in value. This is why it is important to be optimistic and have hope for your financial future.**

Historical stock market returns, such as the *S&P 500 index*, show this potential. This index, which began in 1926, was initially named the Composite Index and started with only 90 stocks. It has since become a barometer or benchmark for tracking the performance of the United States equity market, and in 1957, it was expanded to include 500 stocks. Historical records indicate that the average annual return from 1926 through 2023 was approximately 10%.[1] Over the last four decades, the average yearly return has done even better, averaging over 11%. This index represents approximately 80% of the US stock market's value or capitalization. A company's *market capitalization*, simply put, is its value based on the price of the stock multiplied by all outstanding shares.

The S&P 500 index has increased considerably over the decades and will almost certainly continue to rise over long periods (ten or more years). Consider this: The S&P index was valued at nearly $40 at the end of 1957 and $4,769 at the end of 2023.[2] The average rate of return during this period, including dividends, was over 10.5% per year.[3] By measuring the stock performance of the 500 largest public corporations in the United States, this index provides a secure and reliable representation of the health of the US stock market, thereby serving as a solid basis for future investment. The index calculation is determined by the market capitalization of the companies in the index, divided by an index divisor (determined by the S&P Dow Jones Indices organization).

## Corrections and Crashes, Oh My

Market corrections and crashes are expected, have happened before, and will continue to occur. The S&P 500 has experienced fluctuations yearly for the last ninety-four years, with 27% of those years showing negative results and 73% showing positive returns. Historical evidence indicates that a longer investment period, spanning market highs and lows, generally increases the likelihood of a positive outcome. For example, 94% of ten-year spans have produced positive returns over the past ninety-six years ending in 2023.[4] Investors who weathered occasional declines in stock prices were historically rewarded for their patience and long-term perspective by earning back those losses and experiencing net gains. Investing in the market may be a rocky ride in the short term, but it has consistently increased over time.[5]

The data from Crestmont Research, a firm that provides financial insights and financial market education services, is even more persuasive in demonstrating the importance of time in investing.[6] They studied the rolling twenty-year total returns of the S&P 500, including dividends, from 1900 to 2022. All 104 rolling twenty-year periods experienced positive total returns. This means that whether an investor bought at the market peak or a low point, they would have seen a positive return by simply holding on to an S&P 500 index for twenty years. This extensive data supports a long-term optimistic outcome for the S&P 500 index.

The Dow Jones Industrial Average (DJIA) is another stock market index and includes a much smaller number of companies than the S&P. It follows thirty "blue chip" US companies, the largest and most well-known companies in their industries. Intended to serve as a proxy for the US stock market, the Dow has tracked closely with the S&P.

The elephant in the room is a market crash or correction, during which your stocks drop significantly in value and ruin your dreams. The Dow, for example, closed at 589.64 after a market crash in December 1974, losing about 45% of its value between January 1973 and December 1974.[7] Although it had grown to over 18,000 by the end of 2014, averaging over 12% growth rate annually, investors had to learn the meaning of patience.[8]

If a crash occurs close to or during your retirement, you may be forced to sell a portion of your equity portfolio when it drops in value to meet your financial lifestyle needs. This leaves less of your portfolio intact to recover when the market rebounds, which is more likely if you have invested a significant portion of your portfolio in equities. Looking at this another way, retirement can last for several decades, and you need to protect against running out of money, so investing in equities is important because they have greater growth potential and the ability to beat inflation than fixed-income returns—even if that means needing to deal with the volatility that comes with the territory. Below, we discuss asset diversification to help manage inevitable market fluctuations.

## *Timing the Market Is a Recipe for Disappointment*

Unfortunately, many individuals lose money in the stock market because they seek quick profits and believe they can accurately predict its movements. They try to select individual stocks or funds to make substantial gains quickly. Instead, this approach often leads to buying at high prices and selling at low ones, which is different from conventional investing wisdom. In other words, they buy too late when the market is rising; when it is tanking, they sell too early.

An example of this behavior occurred in 1999 when the Nasdaq (one of the major stock market exchanges) experienced an annual increase of over 85% for the year.[9] Investors continued to buy, setting records for money going into the stock market in the first quarter of 2000 (more dollars going in, fewer dollars going out).[10] In March 2000, the market reached a high, but by October 2002, it had lost 77% of its value, falling from 5,048 to 1,139.[11] Investors started panicking and selling, pouring record-setting amounts into bond funds, a common investment strategy for investors seeking less risk when they pull money from stocks.[12] The problem is that when too much money leaves stocks and is put into bonds, bond prices are pushed higher (and yields go down) due to increased demand.[13] As you can see, equity investors tended to buy very high and sell low, pursuing the wrong strategy.

## OTHER INVESTMENT OPPORTUNITIES

Most 401(k) plans offer several investment options besides the US stock market. Two markets that are attractive to investors include international equities and bonds.

### The International Stock Market

For US investors, stocks of companies outside the United States are considered international. Notably, about 40% of the global market capitalization comprises non-US stocks, so most investors should be exposed to them.[14]

However, there is certainly a healthy amount of debate among experts regarding whether to invest in them. International funds have two main advantages. They offer diversification and the opportunity to outperform US stocks during specific periods.[15] Vanguard, a leading asset management firm, suggests that US investors can benefit from holding international stocks in their portfolios by adding exposure to potentially higher returns. However, like almost all investments, this is not guaranteed and should be approached cautiously.[16] Global stocks can come with higher risks, and some advisors argue that separate exposure to international stocks is unnecessary because many large US companies earn significant revenue internationally.[17]

Many advisors recommend investing 15% to 25% of your portfolio in international stocks.[18] As an example, my portfolio has about 20% international stock exposure through foreign mutual funds that don't hold US equity.

### Bonds and Bond Funds

A bond is similar to a loan, like a mortgage, as it involves borrowed funds and debt repayment with interest. However, in the case of a bond, you are not the borrower. You are the lender, advancing funds to a government or a company (known as the bond issuer), which will repay you with interest and principal over a stated period.

Bonds are viewed as less volatile and more stable than stocks because of their predictability and stability.

- Bonds provide fixed interest payments, making their returns more predictable.
- If a company goes bankrupt, bondholders get paid before stockholders.
- Bonds are generally less influenced by market fluctuations than stocks.

Bonds become more attractive to investors as they age because they preserve the investment portfolio's value, reduce risk, and generate income. These goals are especially important for financial security in retirement. Investing part of your portfolio in bonds and cash allows this portion of your portfolio to better maintain its value in periods of stock market declines and gives your stocks time to recover.

But bonds are not risk-free, and the riskier a bond is, the higher the rate of return should be to compensate for the increased risk. Interest rate and credit risk are two key risks to consider when investing in bonds.

*Interest rate risk:* Rising interest rates are a risk for investors because, when interest rates rise, new bonds can be purchased at higher rates, causing the market value of existing bonds in your portfolio to drop. On the other hand, when interest rates fall, new bonds can be purchased at lower rates, causing the value of existing bonds in your portfolio to rise. Interest rate risk is an issue if you sell bonds before their maturity since the bond's price can be less than what you originally paid due to rising interest rates. For example, if you purchase a $1,000 bond that pays 4% annually and are forced to sell because of an emergency or other reason when new bonds can be purchased at $1,000 and pay 6%, your bond must be sold at a discount (loss) because the new bond is more attractive to investors with its higher yield. You sell the bond for about $800 to make your bond competitive in the market.

The value of your bond or bond fund, whether you own it or plan to purchase it, is important because it affects both the amount you pay and the income you will earn. A bond with a face value, often called a par value, of $1,000 will pay back the $1,000 par value when it matures after its stated life. But it might be available to purchase at a discount of $950 when interest rates are rising, and this means you'll actually earn more—the stated interest *and* the differential between what you paid and what you'll be paid back at maturity. Conversely, the same bond might cost $1,100 if interest rates decrease, reducing the overall return you make on that investment.

The rate of return on a bond, known as its *yield*, is determined by dividing the stated interest payment by the purchase price. If the bond in this example were a one-year bond with a par value of $1,000 and a stated interest rate of 6%, the annual interest payment would be $60. But if you paid a discounted price of $950 for the bond, your yield would be 6.3% ($60 ÷ $950). You would earn the $60 interest and the $50 differential between what you paid for it and the face value you receive upon maturity. But if you bought it at a premium for $1,100, your annual yield would be only 5.5% ($60 ÷ $1,100), and your overall return would actually be a loss (the $100 premium offset by the $60 interest). Understanding how interest rates affect the price of bonds and yields is critical to making wise investment decisions.

*Credit risk:* The possibility that the government entity or company issuing the bonds may be unable to make interest or principal payments when they are due is known as *credit risk* or *bond default risk*. Rating agencies like Moody's and Standard & Poor's (S&P) try to assess the ability of bond issuers to meet their obligations. Then, they assign a credit rating to the issuers. Ratings range from AAA to D. Bonds with AAA (or close to it) are considered very likely to be repaid, while bonds with increasingly lower ratings are more likely to default.

Risks can be mitigated by investing in a bond fund, a diversified portfolio of many bonds. The fund can include bonds from the government, corporations, and other issuers. It minimizes credit and interest rate risks because it invests in many bonds, significantly reducing the possibility of large losses. Interest payments from the bonds in the fund are paid as dividends to the investors, serving as a fixed source of income in your portfolio.

## DIVERSIFICATION AND ASSET ALLOCATION

*Diversification* is spreading your investments across different companies and industries to reduce portfolio risk. For example, investing your portfolio in just one stock carries much more risk because if that company or industry hits hard times, you could suffer major losses. Holding many different stocks, such as the S&P 500, spreads the investments across many companies, helping reduce this risk.

Understanding *asset allocation* is another crucial aspect of your investment strategy. It refers to how your retirement and other investments are spread across different types of assets, such as stocks, bonds, real estate, and cash. Your optimal percentage depends on your time horizon, risk tolerance, financial goals, and so on and will change throughout your life as you get closer to retirement and your risk tolerance and goals change. By understanding this concept, you can take control of your investment strategy and make the decisions that are best for you.

Your *time horizon* refers to when the funds will be invested before they are needed. Deciding how to allocate your funds among the different classes is important because your needs will change. Bonds are less volatile than stocks, but their long maturities can yield lower returns than equity investments. Therefore, younger investors are typically advised to allocate most of their assets to equity, but as retirement approaches, bonds are often recommended as an addition to the portfolio.

For example, if you are beginning your career, you have a long time horizon before you retire and need the funds for retirement, so you have plenty of time to deal with the ups and downs in the equity markets. Therefore, you should invest more in the stock market when you can ride out the bumps. I recommend 100% in the equity markets for at least the first three-quarters of your career, especially if you have a reasonably secure job or feel you can replace it. As you approach retirement, a more conservative allocation with an element of bonds might be suitable to reduce volatility. There are other essential factors to consider when formulating your investment strategy as retirement nears. One key consideration is whether you can work longer, save more, and reduce expenses. If so, you will be in a good position to be more aggressive in your investment strategy as you age. However, if these options are not feasible, you will likely not want to assume too much risk, and a more conservative investment strategy may be appropriate for you.

Your *risk tolerance* refers to how much volatility you are willing to accept. For example, if stocks fall 50%, will you panic and start selling low at precisely the wrong time? Or can you deal with the severe ups and downs in the market, knowing that the market will recover in the long term?

Your *financial goals* refer to the purpose of your savings. In this case, your 401(k) goal is to save for retirement so that you have sufficient funds and flexibility to do the things you want to do when you stop working and live the lifestyle that matches your dreams. Do you plan to travel? Undertake new hobbies? Move to a more or less expensive city? Downsize your home—or buy a second home? Fund your own medical and long-term care needs?

Diversification and asset allocation are personal choices, and no one-size-fits-all rule exists. Finding the right blend is more art than science, and fortunately there are a number of investment vehicles that can help with implementing these strategies.

## INVESTMENT CHOICES

Most 401(k) plans offer a variety of investment options that give participants the ability to choose a strategy that works for them given their goals, tolerance, and timeframe. These options involve funds administered by professionals and allow investors to pool their monies to buy large quantities of equity or bond securities.

### Overview of Mutual Funds

Typically, plans offer ten to twenty mutual funds, and most are *actively managed*. Active management is where fund managers analyze stocks and select investments they believe will outperform a relevant index that measures how well a group of assets perform, such as stocks or bonds. Alternatively, *passive investing* is an approach where the fund's manager buys all (or a sample of) stocks or bonds within a particular index. This type of portfolio is called an *index fund*, and its goal is to mirror the performance of the index on which it is based. The S&P is a well-known index that tracks the performance of five hundred of the largest corporations. The Nasdaq Composite, another well-known index, tracks the performance primarily of technology stocks.

### Actively Managed and Index Funds

The stock market has done very well as a wealth-building tool, and active fund managers aim to beat the indexes. However, it is rare for active managers, including professional investors, to do better than the relevant index over long periods consistently. In addition, actively managed funds tend to be more expensive than index funds, which are more cost-effective with far lower fees than actively managed funds. This, along with the simplicity of index investing, makes these sorts of funds attractive to many investors. They require very little effort, which is fantastic because it frees up your time to focus on your career so you can earn and save more. And by putting the analysis and decision-making responsibility in the hands of professional fund managers, the entire investment process can be much less daunting. We all have busy lives; our time is a precious asset. Because this investment makes the most of it, I am a big fan of index investing.

To further build the case for index funds versus actively managed funds, consider that Morningstar, an investment research company, found actively managed funds have generally failed to survive and beat their S&P comparisons or benchmarks, especially over longer time horizons. Moreover, the S&P Indices Versus Active (SPIVA) scorecards, which compare the performance of actively managed funds to the relevant S&P index and aim to educate investors about whether active managers beat their index benchmarks sufficiently to justify their high fees, have shown that picking stocks individually is a challenging and unreliable strategy. Most active managers underperform their benchmark, particularly over long periods, making a strong indexing case.[19]

Here are some other key findings from the 2023 SPIVA report:

- Over one year, about half of active managers underperform the index.
- The vast majority of actively managed equity funds underperformed over the long term. For example, over ten years, over 80% underperformed their index.
- Even more underperformance was observed over fifteen to twenty years, with more than 90% of active managers underperforming the index.[20]

These statistics highlight the significant challenges of professional investors and indicate that individual investors have very little chance of success when attempting to outperform the market. Moreover, the time and effort required to research and select individual stocks or actively managed funds make it even more unappealing. See appendix A for more detailed information.

Given this information, investing in an index fund is logical and sensible for most investors—especially those investing in 401(k) plans.

**Index funds outperform high-paid, intelligent, and ambitious investment professionals more than 90% of the time over fifteen-to-twenty-year periods, require minimal maintenance, and are remarkably easy to implement.**

For most individual investors, active management does not make sense, and I don't recommend using this strategy.

## Target Date Funds

Another option for investing your funds, especially if you do not want to manage your investments in two or three index funds, is to choose a single fund, known as a *target date fund*. These are good choices because of their simplicity as long as the fees are reasonable. Here, you can invest in just one fund. These funds invest in a blend of stocks, bonds, and other securities and automatically modify their asset allocation as they approach the year the investor plans to retire. See chapter 5 for more information on these funds.

## Annuities

One other investment option to mention is an *annuity*. These contracts are between an investor and a financial institution, such as an insurance company, which offer a secure lifetime (or joint lifetime) income stream. Today, most 401(k) and IRA account holders must decide where to invest their retirement savings over decades, which can be confusing and stressful. Annuities offer a way to provide a specific annual revenue stream at retirement, allowing 401(k) participants to convert all or a portion of their retirement accounts into annual income. In other words, they can exchange their account balance for a paycheck for life.

Unfortunately, fiduciaries of 401(k) plans have historically hesitated to offer annuities as a 401(k) option. They have been concerned about liability they might encounter if they select an insurer to provide the annuity payments and that provider ultimately fails to pay. Over the years, legislation has reduced these liability concerns for 401(k) plans, and annuities can now be offered without liability concerns. Annuities can help free individuals from the many confusing and stressful 401(k) investment decisions and help them avoid outliving their savings due to poor planning or investing.

Sarah is a good example of this. At sixty-five years old, she is ready to stop working, and she is now considering how to manage the $500,000 balance in her 401(k). She wants to ensure she can live well and not run out of money. So she decides to spend $500,000 on an annuity. That money is exchanged for an annuity of $25,000 a year for the rest of her life, *no matter how long she lives*. This lets Sarah know exactly how much she will get every year, and she doesn't have to worry about investing her savings and running out of money. On the other hand, she has a fixed budget, and unexpected expenses or inflation may be a problem unless she has additional funds.

How many employers will add annuity options to their lineup is still being determined. The Plan Sponsor Council of America (PSCA), founded in 1947, is a national nonprofit organization that supports companies sponsoring retirement plans. The organization is dedicated to improving employee retirement outcomes through various initiatives, including research, education, and advocacy. As part of its mission, the PSCA conducts an annual survey on profit-sharing and 401(k) plans to gather comprehensive data on plan design, administration, and participant behavior. This survey is extremely detailed and widely referenced. According to its 66th Annual Survey, approximately 10% of plans offer an annuity, up from 8% as reported in the 65th Annual Survey.[21] This percentage will likely continue to increase over the years. For employees that do have this option, it is worth a look.

## FEES: AN IMPORTANT CONSIDERATION

Fees, often charged as a percentage of holdings in an investment account to cover management and other operating expenses, can significantly affect investment returns. Both actively managed and index (passively managed) funds charge these fees, often presented as expense ratios showing the fee in relation to the total investment. The ratios vary depending on how the funds are managed and the types of investment. According to Morningstar, actively managed mutual fund expense ratios were 0.48% for large-cap US stocks, 0.33% for intermediate-term core bond funds, and 0.62% for foreign large-cap funds. Index fund expense ratios were 0.05% for large-cap US stocks, 0.04% for intermediate-term core bond funds, and 0.11% for foreign large-cap index funds.[22]

So if you invest $20,000 in the three funds shown, the fees that you might pay annually are displayed in table 1.

*Table 1. Fee Comparison: Active vs. Passive*

| Amount or type of investment | Fees as a % of assets | | Dollar amount | |
|---|---|---|---|---|
| | Active (%) | Passive (%) | Active | Passive |
| $10,000 in large-cap stocks | 0.48 | 0.05 | $48 | $5 |
| $5,000 in bonds | 0.33 | 0.04 | $16.50 | $2 |
| $5,000 in foreign stocks | 0.62 | 0.11 | $31 | $5.50 |
| Totals | | | $95.50 | $12.50 |

Fees for active management are over seven times greater! Because they are one of the key reasons that index funds overperform actively managed funds over long periods, fees are very important to consider. Vanguard's late founder, John Bogle, who created the index fund, joked about his creation: "You get what you do not pay for."[23]

## SUMMARY

- The US stock market provides the best long-term growth opportunities for retirement savings. The S&P 500 index has earned an impressive 10% for about one hundred years, from 1926 through 2023.
- Other investment opportunities, including international equities and bonds, help balance risk and market fluctuations.
- Diversity and allocation choices should be based on your financial goals, risk tolerance, and investment horizon.
- Index funds are excellent investments for individual investors because of their wealth-building potential. They also offer low fees, little maintenance, and long-term performance.
- Fees associated with investment options should be considered when making decisions.

# CHAPTER 3

## Managing Your Financial Security, Savings, and Debt

### TIPS AND TOOLS #1: ENSURING YOUR FINANCIAL SECURITY

Live below your means! Yes, that is the most important thing you can do for your financial security because it allows you to save each year. Hopefully, you will get an annual raise and be able to save a portion of it without much pain, freeing up more of your budget for some luxuries and fun. But regardless of your salary level now or going forward, a mindset of financial prudence helps you build wealth and avoid worrying about the future.[1]

Additionally, saving for retirement is a long-term endeavor. It requires patience, sacrifice, and consistency, and at times, you will likely need to tighten your budget, work hard, and make difficult choices that prioritize long-term financial security over short-term indulgences. Most successful people work hard, sacrifice, and are driven to succeed, and you are no different. Think about the basketball legend Michael Jordan. When he started playing in the NBA, he thought his jump shot still needed improvement. So in the offseason, he took hundreds of practice shots a day until it was perfected. Jordan may have had outstanding talent, but he also had the humility to recognize that he had to constantly work at his game to be the best player in the world. The sacrifices you make now will pay off in a secure and comfortable retirement. And who knows? They may even allow you to retire early.

The second critical element of financial security is the accumulation of about six months' living expenses in cash. This should actually be your first step before starting your 401(k) or other savings. Your emergency funds are intended to enable you to pay for expenses if you find yourself out of work or facing unexpected repairs or bills without needing expensive credit cards or loans or having to liquidate investments.

Then, after you've set aside your emergency funds, you can start saving. You can hold index funds in both your tax-advantaged accounts (like a 401(k) or IRA), where you save for retirement, and in your regular taxable investment accounts (such as those you might hold at Charles Schwab or Vanguard), where you save for a down payment on a house, car, vacation, or any other significant purchases or expenses.

> **Financial security is best achieved by living below your means, maintaining an emergency cash fund, and setting aside savings in tax-advantaged and taxable investment accounts.**

## TIPS AND TOOLS #2: HOW MUCH IS ENOUGH?

Saving a million dollars or more is undeniably an impressive feat. But the real question is this: How much do you really need for a peaceful, secure retirement? The answer is complex because it depends on many factors, including your spending habits, healthcare costs, inflation, market performance, longevity, tax rates, and more. Many of these variables are difficult to predict with precision decades into the future, and some are not even within your control.

For example, a small error in assumptions, such as inflation levels or investment returns over decades, can lead to large discrepancies in estimating future needs. The same uncertainty is true for housing costs, which many people overestimate. Despite a rise in housing costs across the country, average housing costs for individuals generally drop over time because people downsize, move to less expensive locations, or pay off their mortgages.

Another factor is healthcare costs. Fidelity estimates that an average sixty-five-year-old couple's healthcare needs will total $300,000 throughout their retirement, and that estimate will certainly increase over time.[2] Of course, issues like chronic illness or longevity could increase those averages significantly, while excellent health can bring these types of financial burdens down.

The only guarantee in predicting future costs, and therefore predicting how much you'll really need, is that *unforeseen challenges will arise*. There is no one method for calculating how much you will need to save for a comfortable retirement, but several approaches are presented below for your consideration.

## Fidelity's 15% Model

Fidelity suggests saving 15% of your income throughout your career for retirement.[3] Their model for calculating an adequate retirement savings portfolio assumes an individual begins saving at this level from age twenty-five onward, invests over 50% of their savings in stocks over their lifetime, retires at sixty-seven, and aims to maintain their preretirement standard of living throughout retirement. The model also assumes you can take an offset against the 15% savings level if your company offers a match. For example, if your 401(k) match is 6%, you have to save only 9% annually.

Fidelity states that, for most people, this level of savings will provide part of the income needed in retirement, with the balance coming from Social Security.[4] Fidelity also notes that your savings rate needs to increase if you want to retire earlier than sixty-seven. For example, a retirement at sixty-five would require a 19% savings rate. Many advisors advocate saving much more—even 50% or more of your income. This is fine as long as you also take advantage of things you enjoy. Try to find the right balance so you can enjoy the ride.

Fidelity also suggests using a simple tool to periodically assess whether your retirement savings are on track based on multiples of your salary and your age.[5] By the time you're thirty years old, for example, you should have accumulated the equivalent of one year's salary.

By age thirty-five, you should have accumulated twice your salary; three times by forty, six times by fifty, and eight times by sixty. By the time you've reached sixty-seven, you should have saved ten times your salary. Then, after retirement, Fidelity suggests withdrawals should be limited to between 4% and 5% of your retirement savings, adjusted for inflation as time passes.

While individual savings opportunities and objectives will vary due to differences in lifestyle, retirement age, and other circumstances, Fidelity's 15% model can serve as a helpful savings guide. If 15% seems like a high threshold, two other strategies, described below, may be more appropriate for you.

### The 4% Rule

A second approach is the so-called 4% rule. This rule suggests setting up your retirement savings to allow for a withdrawal from your retirement portfolio at the rate of 4% each year, with the aim of having the portfolio last through a thirty-year retirement. A study at Trinity University helped establish the rule.[6]

What that means in terms of how much to save is that you can calculate your required savings by dividing your desired annual income in retirement by 4%. For example, if you planned to spend $40,000 annually once you retire, you would need a retirement nest egg of about $1 million ($40,000 ÷ 0.04). This spending amount of $40,000 can be adjusted to account for inflation with a 95% chance of success that you will not outlive your savings. For example, if inflation rises 2% next year, you could give yourself a raise to $40,800 next year. This rule, based on a portfolio with 50% stocks and 50% bonds, has historically (since 1926) ensured that retirees would not run out of money over a thirty-year retirement period.

You can increase your retirement spending if you also have Social Security benefits and other savings. For instance, you can spend $65,000 in your first year of retirement if you have earned a Social Security benefit of $15,000 annually ($40,000 from your retirement savings + $15,000 from benefits).

Although this rule is not precise because, among other things, it is based on projected spending, sometimes decades into the future—

which can be very difficult to predict—it provides a sound, basic method for estimating your ballpark retirement needs. As retirement gets closer, estimating retirement spending will get easier and more precise because you'll have a better idea of your actual spending level and needs.

## Retirement Calculator

The retirement calculator is a third tool that can be used more precisely as you approach retirement. It helps estimate how much money you need to save based on your current age, annual income, income tax rates, expenses, existing savings, monthly contribution, retirement age, life expectancy, preretirement rate of return, postretirement rate of return, inflation rate, annual income increase, and so on.

I have used retirement calculators for decades to help with retirement planning, and I appreciate the precision provided by this approach. Boldin and Pralana are two calculators I found through the website Can I Retire Yet?—a quite informative resource. And while both offer a basic free version, their premium (paid) ones provide more features.[7] By the way, I receive no financial or other benefit from these tools, and there are many other retirement calculators and financial management tools on the market to consider. Of course, you can always hire a financial advisor to help, but they can be expensive, and this expense will diminish your returns.

## The Future Funds Forecast ($F^3$)

While life is meant to be lived and enjoyed, people have different philosophies regarding living in the present versus planning for or worrying about the future. Understanding the long-term impact of daily spending can help people make choices that align with their goals. Living within one's means, avoiding excessive debt, and saving for the future create a financial framework that allows for luxuries without guilt. Treating yourself to a favorite treat—whether it's adopting a puppy, buying daily $5 coffees, or signing up for a $12 monthly subscription—doesn't mean these expenses are bad. A simple calculation can help you weigh the trade-offs and make well-informed decisions. For example, passing up the $5 daily coffee that could grow into tens of thousands of dollars over several decades might motivate someone to spend that money differently on retirement savings or a nice vacation. I encourage readers to review their spending habits and consider the future value of their money if invested.

People face numerous spending decisions daily, from the $5 morning coffee to the $12 monthly subscription services and even larger expenses like car payments, which, according to credit reporting agency Experian, averaged $734 for new cars in the second quarter of 2024.[8] While some of these expenses may seem insignificant or justifiable in isolation, their cumulative effect over time can be substantial. I will highlight the potential wealth accumulated by redirecting these funds into savings and investments.

To illustrate the dollar value of the savings from daily coffee, monthly subscriptions, and car payments over forty years, we'll present the final dollar amounts at an assumed 10% return. This will provide a concrete understanding of the potential financial outcomes of these saving strategies.

Below are the projected saving accumulations if the coffee, monthly subscription, and monthly auto payments are redirected into savings, calculated at a 10% return.

- Coffee savings at 10%: $807,730
- Subscription savings at 10%: $70,105
- Car payments savings at 9%: over $1,000,000 ($250 per month for a car priced at $20,000)[9]

These figures demonstrate the profound impact of saving and investing, even small amounts regularly, over a long period.

My website offers the Future Funds Forecast ($F^3$), a free calculator that you can use to project the accumulations of any expense redirected into savings. You can input the amount of any expense and choose an assumed savings rate and timeframe. I encourage you to use this tool and calculate the future value of the redirected expense before making financial decisions. At the very least, you will realize what you are giving up regarding future savings.

**Before buying an expensive item, consider using the Future Funds Forecast (F³) to evaluate the opportunity cost and make a well-informed decision. The other tools—Fidelity's 15% model, the 4% rule, and retirement calculators—can help minimize the guesswork involved in determining how much is enough as well.**

## TIPS AND TOOLS #3: BEWARE OF DEBT!

Do you dream of a worry-free retirement, where money concerns are a thing of the past? This book is dedicated to turning that dream into a reality. However, debt can derail your best-laid plans. Think of it as the enemy or thief in your wealth-building marathon. I learned about its danger through powerful lessons from my father.

When I was a teenager, my dad, a certified public accountant, advised me of the dangers of high-priced debt. He shared a story about a client who made a very comfortable living, owned beautiful, expensive cars, and enjoyed extravagant vacations. However, despite his significant salary, he could not save due largely to accumulating a mountain of high-priced debt to finance his fancy lifestyle. As he made more money, he increased his spending instead of saving for the future. The more he borrowed to help fund his lifestyle, the further his debt escalated with automobile loans and a large mortgage on his second home.

Through this story and others, my dad taught me that appearances may be misleading and that "you cannot judge a book by its cover." I made a mental note to approach debt with caution and live within my means. I was determined to work hard and progress with my career while maintaining a comfortable lifestyle, saving wisely, and avoiding lavish spending as my earnings increased. Over the years, I have seen many fall into this trap of "lifestyle creep." I have agreed with my dad that it is much more important to have financial resources than to show off your fancy stuff to others so they *think* you are rich—especially if you need to borrow money to acquire all these things.

I sometimes browse Instagram or Facebook when bored, which is rare, and after only a few minutes, I remind myself, yet again, to stay away for good. It seems like everywhere you look, people are showing off their fancy stuff: cars, vacations, boats, bodies, surgeries, or whatever else they can. Why work so hard, have no savings, and live in constant financial stress? To impress others? This lifestyle makes no sense to me. My dad and mom never belonged to the "dress-to-impress club," and I was not interested in joining either. The real-life case study of my dad's client was not just a business lesson. It became a life lesson: Live within your means. Do not buy expensive cars or houses or regularly take excessive vacations. Instead, save for retirement. Avoid spending more just because your income rises. In fact, try to *save more*. If you get a 10% raise, that's great! Save half of it and spend the rest. And, by all means, be wary of debt.

## Credit Cards

Did you know that by the end of the third quarter of 2023, American household debt had soared by $228 billion to a record $17.3 trillion?[10] This increase was primarily caused by increased mortgages, student loan balances, and credit card debt, which grew the fastest, at almost 5% from the previous quarter and more than 16% annually.[11] Cards might seem harmless, offering the convenience of borrowing repeatedly, but they can destroy your finances and planning.

Consider a Visa card with a 20% annual interest on a $4,000 balance. If you are repaying $100 monthly, you would need over five and a half years to extinguish it, with an additional $2,647 in lost interest.[12] It's like pouring money down the drain! With sky-high interest rates, if these debts are not settled (paid in full) each month, they can balloon exponentially. If this debt trap has already captured you, you will need a lot of discipline to eliminate it. But you can do it.

Of course, you should pay off the debt with the highest interest rate first, as these are the most expensive. For example, if you have both credit card debt and student loans, pay the credit cards down first because the interest rates are likely much higher than those on your student loans. Nevertheless, all your debt needs to be repaid as soon as you can, so be diligent and do your best.

## Automobile Loans

Car loans are another type of loan that must be considered carefully. If you do need to finance a car, keep in mind that, in general, you will get more value if you buy a used car because it will depreciate (lose value) less throughout its lifespan than a new vehicle.[13] Used cars are also far less expensive than new cars.

## Mortgages

Not all debt is necessarily bad. Many advisors consider mortgage debt to be "good debt." However, mortgages should be carefully evaluated.

Linda, a good friend, recently had a lovely dinner with my wife and me, and she reminisced about how finances had been an important issue during her youth. Her mother liked to spend, and since money was tight, she used credit cards, accumulating debt. When Linda's parents wanted to buy a new house, she knew it was a bad idea. She explained to her parents that it wasn't just the higher mortgage payments that would be a struggle for them. Owning a larger home would also mean higher taxes and expenses for utilities, insurance, maintenance, furniture, and other items. Linda advised her parents to buy a smaller, more reasonably priced home—in fact, the smallest house that would be comfortable. By the way, Linda was in tenth grade at the time. She went on to study at an Ivy league college and became a financial wiz. This is a good example of being careful with mortgages when purchasing a house. Debt, including a mortgage, will cut into your savings. Remember, sometimes less is more! Although debt can help us achieve our goals, it can also derail our financial security.

**To stay on track, don't let your lifestyle desires lead you into debt. Repay your credit cards, student loans, and car loan debt as soon as possible. Purchase a smaller home to minimize mortgage debt.**

## TIPS AND TOOLS #4: BUILDING A BUDGET

Finding a balance that allows you to enjoy life while working toward your financial goals can lead to a more fulfilling experience. My wife's childhood highlights the challenges—and the rewards—of balancing present-day pleasures with future financial security. Cheryl grew up in a middle-class household where her parents carefully managed their finances. Her mother created the budgets, ensuring the family could save for the future and create memorable experiences and good times.

Cheryl's father, Nat, worked diligently for many decades, and her mother, Carole, joined the workforce after Cheryl and her sister, Marci, reached high school. Together, they made thoughtful financial choices, often setting aside funds for special occasions like holidays and vacations. These priorities allowed the family to create lasting memories without compromising their long-term financial stability.

One example of this careful budgeting was Cheryl's Halloween costumes. Instead of spending money on store-bought outfits, her father designed creative costumes at home. Cheryl fondly remembers one Halloween when she dressed as a light switch and her sister, Marci, as a light. This not only saved money but made the holiday extra special.

Carole also budgeted for experiences that mattered most to the family, including vacations. While many family trips were modest, Cheryl remembers they occasionally splurged on luxurious destinations, such as a high-end resort in Aruba. By carefully planning and budgeting, Cheryl's parents ensured these special moments didn't derail their financial goals but instead added richness to their lives.

These stories illustrate how budgeting can be a powerful tool for achieving balance. Cheryl's parents showed that enjoying life in the present is possible while staying mindful of future needs. By prioritizing what mattered most, they lived a fulfilling life, blending today's pleasures with tomorrow's security.

### Track Your Income and Expenses

Determining your monthly income is the first step in this process. Budgeting apps or spreadsheets can simplify this task by assisting in monitoring income and expenses. For those with a steady job, review your pay stub, which can usually be found online. Multiply your net pay by two if you get paid biweekly or by four if you get paid weekly and so on. If you are an independent contractor and your earnings fluctuate monthly, you can use your earnings for the prior twelve months, subtract the tax payments (tax payments can be found on your Form 1040), and divide by twelve to get a monthly average as a ballpark.

It is important to categorize your expenses into fixed (rent, utilities, groceries) and discretionary (dining out, entertainment) categories. Follow these steps:

1. *Determine fixed required monthly expenses.* List all your expenses, including the following:

    Cell phone bills

    Rent or mortgage

    Internet

    Loans

    Homeowner's or renter's insurance

    Car payments

    Car insurance

    Medical insurance

2. *Determine costs for required monthly expenses that fluctuate monthly, such as home maintenance and repairs.* Since these costs change, calculate the average over the last twelve months. Other examples include the following:

    Groceries

    Insurance paid yearly

    Medical deductible

    Medical copayments and noncovered expenses

    Drugs not covered by insurance

    Public transportation (subways, trains, etc.)

    Personal items

    Haircuts

3. *Determine monthly discretionary amounts.* These will vary depending on your must-have items. Discretionary items can include the following:

   Entertainment (movies, shows, concerts, etc.)
   Streaming services
   Dining out
   Clothing
   Charity
   Gifts
   Gym
   Others (nails, massage, etc.)

4. *Establish goals and convert to monthly goal amounts.* This means determining key financial objectives, such as paying off credit card debt, establishing an emergency fund, and saving for a home. These goals can be short, medium, or long term and are explained below.

**Short-term goals**

These goals are set for one to five years. Examples include an emergency fund, paying off debt, or vacationing. Assume you would like to take a fantastic Alaska or Hawaii vacation cruise in two years. You budget $9,000 for this vacation. You must save about $375 monthly ($9,000 ÷ 24 months). A certificate of deposit (CD) or bank account is an appropriate investment for these monthly savings (see below for investment strategies).

   *An emergency fund* is very important and should cover at least six months of living expenses. It provides resources for unexpected events like job loss or emergencies. This fund should be created as soon as possible before other savings. For example, if your required living expenses (nondiscretionary items) total $25,000 per year, you should have an emergency fund of at least $12,500. To fund it over five years, you will need $208 monthly ($12,500 ÷ 60 months).

### Medium-term goals

These goals are set for six to ten years. Examples include buying a car or home. Assume you would like to purchase a home in six years and need to save $40,000 for a down payment. You must save $556 monthly ($40,000 ÷ 72 months or six years).

### Long-term goals

These goals are set for eleven or more years. An example is retirement savings. For this goal, save as much as possible and aim for 15% of your pre-tax salary after subtracting 401(k) matching contributions.

5. *Input, review, and revise in the app or spreadsheet.* First, input all your monthly income and subtract all your expenses:

    Fixed required monthly expenses (item 1)
    Fluctuating required monthly expenses (item 2)
    Discretionary monthly expenses (item 3)
    Monthly goal amounts (item 4)

    Next, review your income and expenses. If your total expenses exceed your income, you will need to adjust your expenses. You should start with your discretionary items and, if needed, reduce your monthly goal amount. Hopefully, your income will increase over time, and you can save more and add discretionary spending to enhance your life. Try to increase your value at work by learning new skills to increase your income.

    In addition, you should focus on your budgets by reviewing them, tracking your actual expenses against your budgets, and adjusting accordingly. For example, if you budgeted $100 a month for entertainment and spent $175, you will need to monitor this more closely, perhaps weekly, to ensure you don't spend more than $25 a week on this item. Quicken or similar tools can simplify this process. Users input their budgeted amounts and actual spending and then compare them. Be flexible and ready to adjust your strategies based on performance and life changes.

## Invest

Next, let's explore how to invest the monthly amounts you've set aside for your goals (from step 4).

### Short Term (One to Five Years)

For short-term goals, consider using savings accounts or CDs. These investments protect the principal but yield lower returns. This makes sense because it is important to have the funds available when needed, and the stock market is too risky in the short term.

### Medium Term (Six to Ten Years)

Mutual funds are good choices for funding these goals. Growth-focused investments are preferable because your assets have more time to recover from market swings. Mutual funds also offer higher returns to offset inflation over extended periods. Balanced or total-return funds that contain a mix of stocks and bonds are good choices because these funds are less volatile than stock-based portfolios and can provide higher returns than CDs or bonds to counteract inflation.

### Long Term (More Than Ten Years)

Longer-term goals typically allow for a higher risk tolerance, thus creating opportunities in equity mutual funds that can return higher yields. An S&P 500 fund is a good choice for long-term goals.

## SUMMARY

- The best way to achieve financial security is by living below your means.
- You can estimate how much you need to save for retirement using the 15% model, the 4% rule, or a retirement calculator.
- Avoid large or unnecessary debt and pay it off as soon as possible.
- Budgeting is important because it helps you manage your assets effectively, live within your means, save for future goals, and reduce financial stress.

# PART II

Opportunities

# CHAPTER 4

## Opportunity One—Participate, Participate, Participate

How would you like to retire with $1 million or even more? Most of us would jump at that chance, but achieving this milestone requires careful planning, smart financial decisions, and sacrifice. The word *retirement* conjures up many different emotions—hope, happiness, anxiety, and fear. For some, it seems like a long-awaited dream, while others worry they may never have enough money. Regardless of your aspirations, financial resources will make them easier to achieve and provide flexibility. Your first step in accumulating these resources is participating in your company's retirement plan, one of the most effective ways to save.

The most common retirement plan is the 401(k). Other defined contribution plans include the 403(b) and the 457(b). These plans are very similar to the 401(k); a key difference relates to the type of employer and employees. Whereas 401(k) plans are typically sponsored by private-sector, for-profit companies like Google or Microsoft, 403(b) plans are for tax-exempt organizations like hospitals, universities, and public schools, and 457(b) plans cover government employees. No matter which type of retirement plan your employer offers, you need to get started!

## BE IN IT TO WIN IT

Taking the right steps can prepare you for a financially secure future. So let's explore how to do this with a simple case study. Don, a wise young man, began contributing to his 401(k) plan early in his career. By being frugal, Don consistently contributed $100 per week, about $5,000 annually. Over forty years, Don accumulated over $2 million, made possible by an average S&P annual return of 10% (the average S&P total annual return from 1928 through 2023). Of course, everyone has a unique lifestyle and financial philosophy, and all are valid. Some methods, like Don's, focus on frugality and consistent saving, which helped him reach his goals more quickly. Different strategies may work better for others based on their unique circumstances and preferences.

Also, the potential for retirement savings is even more impressive for those fortunate enough to receive a 50% match on their annual contribution. If that had been the case for Don and his match was $2,500 per year, his account balance after forty years would be about $3.3 million.

As the lotto jingle goes, "You got to be in it to win it!" Starting early and staying consistent are the keys.

## DON'T DELAY!

Let's consider a scenario where Don would have started contributing later in his career for just sixteen years, the average number of years participants contribute to their retirement plans.[1] Assuming he made the same $5,000 contribution, earned 10% a year, and received the 50% match on his $5,000 annual contribution, he would have accumulated about $269,000. That's over $3 million, or 91%, less than if he'd started in his mid-twenties! Yes, you read that right—*over $3 million less.* The difference is staggering and proves that it is wise to start contributing to your 401(k) as early as possible.

These examples assume a constant annual contribution. However, during your career, you will likely receive salary increases, and if you increase your contributions, subject to plan and legal limitations, you will accumulate even more funds. This power is in *your* hands, and with intelligent investment choices, consistent contributions, and time, you can create significant wealth and enjoy your future in whatever manner is most meaningful to you. And the earlier you start, the greater your financial rewards will be.

## THE MAGIC OF COMPOUNDING

Long-term investing is important for generating large returns partly because of the power of *compounding*.

**By leaving your contributions and the income you earn on those investments in the market for long periods—often decades—you allow these returns to be reinvested and earn additional amounts. This creates an effect like a snowball where the value of your investment grows exponentially over time.**

For example, if you invest $1,000 at an annual return rate of 7%, you will earn $70 in the first year, bringing your total balance to $1,070 at the end of that year. In the second year, you earn 7% again, not on your initial $1,000 but on the $1,070, resulting in a return of nearly $75. This process repeats each year, and the growth becomes substantial over decades. While that might not sound significant after one year, the power of compounding becomes much more evident after numerous years. After forty years, your balance would have grown to approximately $14,975, and the initial principal of $1,000 would become dwarfed by the compounded returns of $13,975. This exponential growth over time highlights the importance of investing early to maximize the growth of your investments.

Returning to the previous scenario, note that Don began investing in his 401(k) forty years ago at $5,000 per year and his company matched his contribution at 50%. The total amounts contributed were, therefore, just $300,000 ($200,000 from Don and $100,000 from his employer), but his balance mushroomed to well over $3 million because of the compounding factor.

Next, imagine you are using the power of compounding even more aggressively and stashing away $15,000 annually. With a steady 10% return over forty years, you would be looking at more than $6,600,000—and that is without any employer-matching contributions. Add a conservative employer match of $2,000 annually at the same growth rate, and you are saving nearly $925,000 more. The total? A mere *$7,525,000!*

Saving $15,000 per year in your 401(k) can seem daunting, especially if you earn $80,000 or even less in annual salary. However, a 19% contribution ($15,000 savings ÷ $80,000 salary) still leaves you with $65,000 before taxes to live on. It demands sacrifice, yes, but think about that end goal! I understand that this level of savings is unattainable for many, but if you can pull it off, you will be handsomely rewarded.

## SUMMARY

- **Participate in your 401(k) or other retirement plan opportunities at the highest level you can afford.**
- **Start saving for retirement as early as possible.**
- **Recognize that the power of compounding can significantly improve your savings over long periods.**

# CHAPTER 5

## Opportunity Two—Invest with Intent

Congratulations, you committed to participate in your company's 401(k) plan! Now what? You need to put that money to work so it can grow. But don't panic—investing doesn't have to be a daunting task requiring complex spreadsheets and financial wizardry. A simple, low-cost, index-based approach can work wonders for you. We will introduce and explore a simple 401(k) investment strategy that, over the long term, will likely yield impressive results with minimal effort. You can also use this approach for your non-401(k) investments in taxable brokerage accounts.

Throughout my career, I have seen many participants make mistakes. Sometimes, they adopt an overly conservative approach, allocating most of their assets to bond funds, even when they are young and have full careers ahead of them. My friend Dan did this, and when he asked me what I thought of his 401(k) portfolio, three-quarters of which was invested in fixed-income funds (bonds), I told him that it looked like the portfolio of a ninety-year-old instead of a man in his thirties, because it was unnecessarily conservative. Others invest in far too many funds, hoping that by casting a wide net, they will get lucky and stumble on a few winners. Still others chase after the hottest funds, mindlessly pursuing recent top performers without considering the fees or other essential selection criteria—only to be disappointed by these funds.

There are several ways to achieve your financial goals: Earn more, reduce expenses, and invest well. Here, the focus is on *investing well*. My approach requires patience and the ability to select low-cost index funds in your 401(k), which most plans offer.[1] Let's meet the funds now.

## START STRONG WITH TWO FUNDS

Imagine starting with two mutual funds for most of your career and *outperforming* seasoned investment professionals. Then, decades later, you might consider adding a third fund to the mix because adjusting your investment strategy as you approach retirement makes good sense. A bond index fund, for example, can be added to your portfolio as you age to help mitigate risk and reduce the volatility that comes with a 100% stock-based portfolio.

> **By starting with two mutual funds, you will likely enjoy excellent returns over many decades and be on solid ground when that retirement day comes. Simplicity matters a lot, and this strategy delivers that—and more.**

### First Fund: Domestic Equities

Your first fund should hold about 80% of the equity in your 401(k) portfolio during the first three-quarters of your career, and a single S&P 500 index fund is an excellent choice for this investment. This provides easy diversification across various industries because you buy 500 of the largest US publicly traded companies, known as *large-cap* and *mid-cap* companies.[2] Many retirement plans offer S&P 500 index funds often established by brokerage firms such as Fidelity, Vanguard, or Schwab.

If your plan offers a *total stock market index fund*, you should consider it because it offers slightly greater diversification. This fund is similar to owning the whole US equity market with one fund and typically consists of thousands of publicly traded companies, including small-cap companies (with valuations between $250 million and $2 billion) and micro-cap companies (with valuations of less than $250 million), neither of which are included in the S&P 500 index. The returns enjoyed by total stock market index funds are similar to those of the S&P 500 index funds, especially over three or more years, even though they track a different index, partly because there is considerable overlap in the stocks.[3] Indexes tracked by total stock market index funds include the Center for Research Security Prices (CRSP) US Total Market Index, Russell 3000 Index, Wilshire 5000 Index, Dow Jones US Total Stock Market Index, S&P US Total Market, or the Dow Jones US Stock Market.[4] Importantly, these funds often charge some of the lowest fees in the investing marketplace.

Unfortunately, based on my experience, total stock market index funds are less common in 401(k) plans than S&P 500 index funds. And some plans don't offer the S&P 500 index funds either. If you do not have access to these, try to pick the fund most similar to the S&P, such as a large-cap index fund, if the fees are reasonable. Look for expense ratios in the range of 0.02% to 0.08%.[5]

If your plan doesn't offer index funds, consider a target date fund (discussed below) or contact your plan administrator or committee to request a fund lineup change to add low-cost index funds. Appendix D shows that roughly 85% of plans offer a US index fund. Significant litigation regarding 401(k) plan investment options and high fees has occurred over the years, adding pressure on the plan's fiduciaries to improve the lineup to reduce fees, address liability concerns, and help participants. The fiduciary ultimately responsible for the plan's administration and the investment of its assets is generally a committee of five to ten members. This committee continually reviews the investment options to ensure they meet basic benchmarks. If not, they may search for an appropriate replacement. In fact, during my career, I have advised many 401(k) plan committees and have found that all are open to discussing the addition of funds and participant concerns, particularly if data supports the inclusion of a particular fund or there is a gap in the lineup that should be addressed.

## Second Fund: International Equities

For US investors, stocks of companies outside the United States are considered international, and your second fund should be a low-cost international index fund that does not include any US companies, such as one that tracks the Financial Times Stock Exchange (FTSE) Global All Cap ex US Index. This index consists of global large-, mid-, and small-cap stocks, excluding US equities. Another index to look for is the Morgan Stanley Capital International All Country World Index (MSCI ACWI) ex USA Index. This one also tracks global stock market performance, excluding the US equities. If your plan does not offer a suitable fund, you can go without international exposure, or you can use your nonretirement investments in taxable accounts or an IRA to invest in these types of funds if you have these assets. Look for expenses ranging from 0.05% to 0.17%.[6] International index funds are recommended because they often outperform actively managed international equity funds, in both the short and long term.[7]

## Third Fund: Bonds

A fixed-income allocation makes sense for most investors as they approach retirement because of the stability this type of asset affords. And, as with equity investments, a *bond index fund* is also the best approach for most investors because of its diversification, simplicity, and low fees. The long-term trend shows that many actively managed bond funds underperform their passive benchmarks. There are periods, however, where actively managed bond funds outperform their passive benchmarks.[8]

This type of fund can provide exposure to various US bonds. Although individual bonds are not generally offered in 401(k) plans, many do offer a domestic bond index fund, which is the way to go as long as the expense ratio is reasonable. According to the 66th Annual Survey, nearly 53% of all 401(k) plans have a domestic bond index fund, and 72% of plans with over 5,000 participants contain this option.[9] In other words, this will likely be available to you if you work at a medium-to-large organization. When assessing these funds, look for expense ratios ranging from 0.02% to 0.08%.[10] Although indexed funds are generally recommended, actively managed bond funds are available in 75% of plans, and it may be appropriate for you if the fees are reasonable (in the range of 0.2% to 0.45%). Or you might consider a target date fund if the fees are unreasonable or you do not have this option in your plan.

The time to move a portion of your portfolio into bonds is generally when you reach age fifty-five to sixty and still have five to ten more years of work. I recommend allocating 25% of your portfolio to bonds at that time. If you are more risk-averse or plan to retire early, you can certainly allocate to bonds at a younger age or at a higher allocation percentage. However, if you are in good health and have time as an ally, you will benefit from retaining a significant equity portfolio for much of your career.

Once you do stop working, consider increasing your bond holdings more to achieve a 60/40 equity to fixed-income split. If you have saved aggressively over the years and can project a comfortable lifestyle going forward into retirement, you might be able to scale back your equity exposure even further to avoid unnecessary risk. Importantly, do not hold tax-free bond funds, such as municipal bonds, in a 401(k) account or IRA because they pay lower returns to compensate for their tax advantage, which is not needed in a 401(k) or IRA.

Another approach is to keep four to five years of living expenses in bonds while maintaining a six-month cash emergency fund. Allocating roughly 25% or 40% of your portfolio to bonds and an emergency fund is a guideline that may cover this level of living expenses. However, the amount will vary based on your needs. Keeping a cash emergency fund and bonds to cover living expenses for extended periods provides financial stability during periods of market underperformance. These funds help ensure access to cash and bonds, reducing the need to sell equity investments at a significant loss. According to Morningstar, historical data shows that the S&P 500 has taken an average of six months to recover from past declines, although the maximum recovery has taken about six and a half years.[11] The idea is to have sufficient resources to navigate most market contractions.

## TARGET DATE FUNDS: AN ELEGANT ONE-STOP SOLUTION

A *target date fund* invests in a mix of stocks, bonds, and other securities and automatically adjusts its asset allocation as it approaches a target date. Generally, the target date is the year the investor plans to retire, and these funds are popular, for good reason. As you age, the fund's automatic adjustment normally becomes more conservative and allocates a greater portion of your portfolio to bonds because, while younger people can afford to take more risks, people approaching retirement should become more conservative with their assets. If your plan does not have index funds available, or if you want even more simplicity than indexing, this might be right for you.

There are several important factors to think about when considering a target approach for your portfolio. First, check how the fund shifts its asset allocation from stocks to bonds over time. Make sure you are comfortable with this adjustment. For example, evaluate whether it is too conservative due to a higher concentration of fixed income throughout your life than is ideal for your situation. Some funds lower their equity allocation to zero by the time retirement age is reached. Others continue to hold some equity positions after the target retirement date. Understanding the differing equity and fixed-income allocations over time and at retirement is important.

Next, compare the expense ratios in the fund you're considering with other target date funds for reasonableness. Lower fees will help you retain more investment returns, so look for expense ratios in the range of 0.05% to 0.35%.

You'll want to review the success of the target date fund in question. Study the historical performance, but understand that past performance doesn't guarantee future results. Finally, you'll also need to consider the reputation and track record of the fund provider, as those with a strong history in target date funds may offer more reliable options. This information can usually be found on your plan's portal.

The target date approach does not offer investors control over their investment or allocation options, and it is primarily for this reason that I prefer the two or three index fund approach discussed above. Asset allocation can be a very personal decision, and there may be important reasons to take on more or less risk based on individual circumstances, which cannot easily be accomplished in a target date fund. If you decide to use the target date approach, you will not have to worry about rebalancing your portfolio, which is discussed next, because it is automatically adjusted over time for you. Fortunately, many 401(k) plans offer automatic rebalancing.

## REBALANCE YOUR PORTFOLIO

Your portfolio's asset allocation naturally shifts as the value of your stocks and bonds fluctuate. Rebalancing refers to the process of selling stocks and buying bonds (or vice versa) to return to your desired allocation. This helps you achieve your desired goal, but it also enables you to sell high, buy low, and profit from successful and intentional investment strategies. According to the 66th Annual Survey, 83% of plans offer automatic rebalancing, whereby your portfolio is adjusted based on the allocation you select, usually yearly or semiannually.[12] If you have an automatic rebalancing feature, I encourage you to use it and further simplify your life!

Assume you reach fifty-five and decide to allocate 25% of your $600,000 portfolio (or $150,000) to a bond fund and 75% of your $600,000 portfolio (or $450,000) to equities with an 80/20 split between US and international stocks. Your portfolio would look like this:

- Bond fund (25% of $600,000): $150,000
- Equity (75% of $600,000 portfolio): $450,000
- US index fund (80% of $450,000): $360,000
- International index fund (20% of $450,000): $90,000

After one year, the portfolio grows and is worth $650,000. The new allocations, shown below, reflect that the US fund returned 15%, the international fund lost 10%, and the bond fund increased 3.3%.

- Bond fund: $155,000
- Equity: $495,000
- US index fund: $414,000
- International index fund: $81,000

To rebalance to your initial desired allocations, you would sell some of your US funds, which had earned an impressive 15%, and use those funds to rebalance your international investments, which had lost value. In other words, you would *sell the US assets high and buy more international assets low.* You would also use some of the domestic equity gains to buy additional bonds; even though the bond fund value had increased nominally, its allocation as a percentage of your total portfolio had dropped. The new allocations would look like this:

- Bond fund (25% of $650,000): $162,500
- Equity (75% of $650,000 portfolio): $487,500
- US index fund (80% of $487,500): $390,000
- International index fund (20% of $487,500): $97,500

Rebalancing is easy and can be done without tax implications or expensive advisors. And after you've completed the exercise, you can sit back and let the stock market continue to do its job. Although there will be ups and downs, and you must weather the storms (financially and emotionally), you will likely be in great shape in the long run.

## SUMMARY

- **Build a great portfolio with three funds: domestic equity, international equity, and bonds.**
- **Consider target date funds for simplicity.**
- **Maximize your success through periodic rebalancing.**

# CHAPTER 6

## Opportunity Three—Use a Smart Roth Strategy

You have taken the first step by deciding to participate in your 401(k) at a level that suits you. However, essential decisions lie ahead, such as choosing between a traditional 401(k) or a Roth contribution or dividing your contributions between a Roth and a traditional one. Throughout my life, during business and law school, I've focused on minimizing and deferring tax payments, even researching and implementing complex strategies to achieve this objective for clients. Choosing to make a Roth contribution can seem counterintuitive for someone focused on tax strategy because it results in paying taxes on your earnings *upfront*, thereby accelerating your tax payments rather than deferring them. But the wisdom behind this strategy will soon be explained.

Years ago, I arrived in New York City after a two-hour train ride from Philadelphia just as it began to pour. As I stepped outside, vendors were selling umbrellas. "Umbrellas, umbrellas! Sir, would you like an umbrella?" I thought it would be worth the purchase if the umbrella could survive my short walk to the subway and another brief walk to my final destination. So I bought one. But within minutes, a gust of wind tore the fabric off, leaving me unprotected from the downpour.

Shortly after that experience, I bought a high-quality umbrella from a reliable manufacturer. Now, every time it rains and my umbrella withstands the storm, I'm glad I paid much more for it upfront. Similarly, although a Roth contribution *accelerates* tax payments rather than deferring them, it can still be a wise investment in the right circumstances and to prepare you for the future, just like that sturdy umbrella. By the way, I still sometimes see poor souls buying those cheap umbrellas, and I observe the inevitable demise shortly after the first minor wind comes along following their purchase. It seems that tried-and-true lessons need to be taught over and over again as new people come along. This chapter will help you avoid that sort of frustration and arm you with the necessary knowledge and strategies to make the right decision as you continue on your journey as CEO of your retirement security.

Despite the tax implications, Roth 401(k) features are pervasive. Indeed, according to the 66th Annual Survey, 89% of all 401(k) plans offer Roth options.[1] Surprisingly, according to the same survey, only 21% of eligible employees take advantage of them. Let us find out if the other 79% are missing out. But first, some background.

Roth contributions are made from after-tax income, which means you pay taxes on the salary or wages contributed to your plan account. But you will enjoy tax-free *growth* in your Roth account, both federal and generally state, as opposed to standard savings or investment accounts where you pay taxes on earnings yearly. When it comes time to withdraw funds in the future, you will not owe *any* federal (and generally state) income taxes, provided it has been at least five years since your first contribution. Note, however, a 10% *penalty tax* will generally be applied if you withdraw funds from your Roth account before you become fifty-nine and a half years old. There are some exceptions for death, disability, or certain one-time home purchases up to $10,000. It is important to note that Roth contributions do not offer a current income tax deduction for the contribution. The tax-free investment growth on earnings and tax-free distributions makes the Roth option advantageous for many individuals.

On the other hand, contributions to a traditional 401(k) plan offer immediate tax advantages through a tax deduction that reduces your taxable income by the amount of your contribution. Also, while the income you accumulate in both your Roth and traditional accounts remains tax-free, you must pay taxes on the distributions you withdraw from your traditional 401(k). It's a matter of your preference to pay taxes now or later. So how do you decide which is best?

Before we address that question, keep in mind that there are limits to how much you can contribute to a 401(k) plan. In 2024, the maximum you could contribute to any 401(k) plan, including Roth and traditional contributions, was $23,000 unless you were fifty or older. In that case, you could make an additional *catch-up contribution* each year of $7,500, increasing your total allowable contribution to $30,500 annually to your combined Roth and traditional accounts.

## WHEN TAXES ARE LOW, GO ROTH; WHEN HIGH, GO TRADITIONAL

The decision on whether to go Roth or traditional can be confusing, but the first place to start is to try and estimate your income and tax rates in retirement. Generally, you will want to contribute to Roth accounts when the income or rates are lower now than later to minimize your tax liability. But it can be difficult to accurately determine tax rates and income levels decades in the future to predict when taxes will be high or low.

Let us consider an example involving a young man, Gene, with whom I have played pickleball. Gene was twenty-four and had just started his career when I decided to take advantage of this teaching opportunity regarding personal finance and 401(k) plans.

Gene's average income tax rate was 15%, and he could afford to contribute $10,000 per year to his company's 401(k) plan. When he asked whether to choose a traditional or Roth contribution, I explained that if he opted for a Roth contribution, 15% of that contribution, or $1,500, would be deducted from his pay now as a tax payment. The remaining $8,500 ($10,000 − $1,500) would be contributed to the Roth 401(k). That $8,500, and its associated earnings over time, would never be subject to taxes again (provided Gene would meet the five-year rule mentioned above). Assuming a 7% interest rate over thirty years, Gene's net after-tax accumulation would amount to $64,705.[2]

In contrast, if Gene made a traditional 401(k) contribution of $10,000, the total amount would be contributed directly to the plan since taxes are deducted upon future withdrawals, not on the initial contribution. This $10,000 contribution and its associated earnings would grow to $76,123 in thirty years, which of course is higher than the Roth accumulation. But it would be subject to taxes of $11,418 ($76,123 × 0.15) upon distribution, assuming he is still in the 15% income tax bracket at that time. His net after-tax accumulation would be $64,705 ($76,123 – $11,418).

Yes, the savings are exactly the same! But that is true only as long as his *tax rate at the time of contribution* is the same as the *tax rate at distribution*. This example made it easy for me to explain to Gene that the decision between Roth and traditional contributions ultimately boils down to tax rates. I advised him to choose the option that leaves him with more money after paying income tax, maximizing his net after-tax accumulation.

Let's change the example to assume that Gene's average income tax rate in retirement is 32%, and he chooses a traditional contribution; everything else in the example is the same. See tables 2 and 3 for examples of Roth and tradition 401(k) contributions.

*Table 2. Roth contribution—Tax paid when contribution made*

| | |
|---|---|
| Roth contribution made (after tax) | $8,500 |
| Roth contribution in 30 years at 7% | $64,075 |
| Tax rate at contribution (now) | 15% |
| Tax on contribution | $1,500 (10,000 × 15%) |
| Income tax on distribution (30 years later) | 0 |
| Net after-tax accumulation | **$64,705** |

*Table 3. Traditional 401(k) contribution—Tax paid at distribution*

| | |
|---|---|
| Traditional contribution made (before tax) | $10,000 |
| Traditional contribution in 30 years at 7% | $76,123 |
| Income tax rate at distribution (30 years later) | 32% |
| Income tax at distribution (30 years later at 32%) | $24,359 ($76,123 × 0.32) |
| Net after-tax accumulation | **$51,764** ($76,123 – $24,359) |

This revised example shows that Gene did not make the correct choice because his net after-tax accumulation is $12,941 ($64,705 – $51,764) less than if he made a Roth contribution instead of the traditional contribution when his tax rate was 15%. But that is true only as long as his tax rate at the time of contribution is lower than the tax rate at distribution.

> **If the tax rate at the time of contribution is less than the assumed rate at retirement, opt for a Roth and pay less tax on the contribution. If the tax rate at the time of contribution is projected to be more than at the time of distribution, opt for traditional and pay less tax at distribution. There is no difference if the tax rate is the same at the time of contribution and distribution.**

## TAKE ADVANTAGE OF OTHER ROTH BENEFITS

Roth contributions offer other potential advantages, which may help tip the scale. First, while both types of contributions often can be withdrawn after age fifty-nine and a half with no penalties (check your plan's SPD to make sure), the fact that Roth withdrawals are tax-free can come in handy if you have to face significant expenses, such as a health crisis, that would lead to large withdrawals that would be taxable if coming from a traditional account.

Second, traditional 401(k) contributions generally require you to take minimum distributions after a certain age (currently age seventy-three and after 2033 seventy-five), but Roth contributions don't have this requirement. This can be a significant advantage to those who wish to leave assets to their children or other beneficiaries or who can otherwise afford to leave their money in the 401(k) account for as long as possible.

Third, Medicare premium rates depend on income levels. These may increase if you take required minimum distributions from a traditional 401(k) plan because those distributions are considered taxable income for tax and Medicare premium calculations. Alternatively, distributions from a Roth account will not affect your premiums be-cause they aren't considered taxable income. Always consult with your accountant or advisor before making a decision.

## DIVIDE YOUR EGGS BETWEEN TWO BASKETS

At the start of a career, the future can seem like a vast ocean. How can you forecast your retirement income from various income sources like pensions, Social Security, 401(k), IRA taxable distributions, and investment earnings? Or how can you predict tax rates when future tax laws may change? Gene and I discussed all this, and we devised a relatively simple strategy that can help many people hedge their bets: You put your eggs in *both* baskets by *splitting* your contributions be-tween Roth and traditional 401(k)s.

If you are a young adult in a low-income tax bracket (say 15% to 20% or less) and anticipate your income rising in the future, opt for Roth at least until about age thirty or until your income, and corre-sponding tax rate, begin to increase significantly. Between the ages of thirty and forty-five, when your income and taxes are rising, con-sider a 50/50 split between Roth and traditional. For example, if you put $10,000 into a 401(k) every year, divide it evenly between the two with $5,000 going into a Roth plan and $5,000 into a traditional one. Then, once you reach forty-five and are in your peak earning years, and facing the high tax rates, consider leaning more toward traditional contributions, with perhaps a 75/25 split. This allows you to defer your taxes when rates are high until retirement, when, for most people, in-come and corresponding tax rates drop.

## IN-PLAN CONVERSION

Another way to hedge your bets is to hold a portion of your contribu-tions in a traditional account, thereby deferring taxes on those earn-ings until a later date and then converting them to a Roth account within the plan later. You should check your plan's SPD to determine whether Roth in-plan conversions are allowed and, if so, whether you may also transfer vested matching contributions. There are a number of reasons a conversion could be beneficial:

1. *Lock in the current tax rates:* This strategy can be beneficial if your income suddenly drops significantly in a year and you think your tax rate will increase significantly in the future. For example, your income decreases due to a job loss, but you expect to be reemployed soon. As we have learned, when tax rates are low, go Roth.

2. *Market correction or crash:* Under this strategy, consider converting if the market dives. For instance, if your $100,000 traditional account suffers a 30% correction and drops to $70,000, you would be taxed on the lower amount of $70,000, not $100,000 or more when the market recovers and you begin your retirement withdrawals. For example, if you are in a 20% bracket, you will pay $14,000 in tax ($70,000 × 0.20) at the time of conversion rather than $20,000 ($100,000 × 0.20) at the time of withdrawal, assuming the market recovered. This means $6,000 saved in taxes. If your tax rate at withdrawal is higher than at conversion, you will save even more.

3. *Guarantee tax-free withdrawals:* As we have already seen, withdrawals from Roth accounts are tax-free, so transferring the funds there makes sure future withdrawals are never taxed.

4. *Manage diversity:* By holding both traditional and Roth accounts, you are diversifying your assets and setting up the ability to manage your taxable income in retirement so that withdrawals can be tailored to your situation.

In short, making the most of your retirement savings does not have to be complicated. With some strategy and flexibility, you can navigate the complexities of retirement planning.

One thing to keep in mind when considering an in-plan conversion is the tax implications of doing so. The amount converted is considered taxable income, and you will be required to pay taxes on that amount in the year of the conversion. Be sure to consider federal, state, and local income taxes that apply and make sure the conversion does not push you into a higher federal income tax bracket.

The good news, though, is that withdrawals from the Roth account will be tax-free if the Roth 401(k) account is at least five years old. However, each Roth conversion has a separate five-year holding period for determining whether the 10% penalty tax applies for withdrawals before age fifty-nine and a half.

A backdoor Roth IRA, covered in chapter 14, is a strategy that can sometimes help individuals reach their financial goals more quickly by making nondeductible contributions to a traditional IRA and converting those contributions to a Roth IRA. A similar strategy is available within 401(k) plans, called the *mega backdoor Roth*. This method allows 401(k) participants to contribute much more to their 401(k) plan by making *after-tax contributions* (funds that are already taxed) and then converting those contributions into a Roth account within the plan.

Participants can significantly increase their total 401(k) contributions by using these after-tax contributions, providing a powerful way to boost Roth savings beyond traditional 401(k) contribution limits.

**2024 Contribution Limits:**

- Pre-tax or Roth contributions limit: $23,000
- Pre-tax or Roth contributions *plus* after-tax contributions and employer contributions limit: $69,000
- For 2024, individuals aged fifty and over can contribute an additional $7,500, for a total of $30,500 in pretax and Roth contributions and $76,500 in all types of contributions

Not all 401(k) plans permit this strategy because after-tax contributions or in-plan 401(k) conversions are optional plan features and may not be allowed. Review your SPD and speak with your plan representatives to determine whether your plan offers this feature. If you confirm this feature is available, continue reading for additional information.

One important consideration is that when after-tax contributions are withdrawn, any earnings will be subject to ordinary income taxes. To avoid this, convert the 401(k) after-tax amounts into a Roth 401(k) through an in-plan Roth conversion as soon as possible after the conversion to minimize taxable earnings. Taxes need to be paid on any earnings that are converted. Taxes are not paid on the after-tax contributions because they have already been paid. Check with your plan to make sure the plan allows this; if not, you will have to wait until you terminate to convert your after-tax amounts and related taxable earnings.

Let's assume Johnson is forty-six years old and has contributed $23,000 in pre-tax or Roth contributions. Johnson's employer contributed $10,000 in matching contributions. Johnson is eligible to make after-tax contributions of $33,000. Executing the conversion as soon as possible minimizes taxable earnings on the contributed amount.

This feature can be particularly helpful for high-income individuals because it enables them to make additional Roth contributions annually. Most individuals cannot afford to maximize these contributions. However, if you can afford to make additional contributions and your plan offers this feature, it is a great opportunity to consider.

Mega backdoor Roth features are complicated, so you should consult with your tax advisor for advice related to your situation.

## SUMMARY

- **Roth 401(k) accounts offer significant tax deferral and reduction opportunities. They can also be a good source of tax-free emergency funding.**
- **If you expect taxes to decrease in retirement, you will likely be better off with a traditional plan. If you expect taxes to increase in retirement, you may be better served by a Roth plan.**
- **By dividing your annual 401(k) contribution between traditional and Roth plans, you can hedge your bets.**
- **An in-plan conversion gives you a second chance at investing in a Roth plan, especially when income or the market drops.**

# CHAPTER 7

## Opportunity Four—Maximize Your Match

Congratulations! You have now made many important decisions about your retirement plan, including participation, investment selection, and type of contribution. It is now time to make sure your *match is being maximized*. If not, you may even change your contribution level to maximize the match.

Finding a great deal can take a lot of time and effort. My friend Sherry, a careful consumer, is skilled at this. She does a lot of research in her quest for value before buying a product, and she loves finding a great deal by balancing quality and price. Her favorite time of year is Thanksgiving, and Sherry enjoys the traditions that bring people together: food drives, the Thanksgiving Day parade, football, and turkey. And then, of course, there is Black Friday. Sherry plans for weeks—scanning ads, making lists, and adding items to her digital cart—hoping to buy products at fantastic prices. On the big day, she wakes up early and is among the first customers to enter her favorite stores. She is thrilled whenever she finds great deals and can save on things she wants and needs.

The 401(k) match is free money, like getting a great deal on something you have been waiting to buy at the right price. But it provides a greater financial benefit because it can improve your financial health throughout your career, while Black Friday happens only once per year. The match is always on sale! Let's make sure you make the most of it.

According to the 66th Annual Survey, over 95% of 401(k) plans offer matching contributions.[1] This is great news; you likely have a match in your plan. The trick is figuring out how to take full advantage of this opportunity and ensure you receive the maximum benefit of the matching contribution.

First, let us step back and learn about the 401(k) match and its calculation. A match is a contribution your company makes to your account *as a reward for your contribution to your own account*. The matching contribution costs you nothing because the company pays for it. However, you must contribute to your 401(k) to receive the company's portion. It is an optional feature offered at the discretion of your employer, and while most things in life are not free, the company match is an exception to this general rule if your company offers one.

And it's simple: Your company fully or partially matches your contribution, up to a percentage of your compensation. The match is usually made pre-tax, which means you don't pay taxes on that income until you later withdraw money from your account, although some employers have chosen to make their match after tax on a Roth basis (as discussed at the end of this chapter).

## HOW IT WORKS

Let's take a look at an example of a match where the plan states the employer will match 50% of the employee's contribution, limited to 6% of compensation. This is known as a *partial matching formula* because the employer matches only a portion (50%) of the employee's contribution. If the employee contributed the full 6% allowed, the employer's contribution would be 3% (0.50 match × 0.06 contribution = 3% match). In this situation, the employee has maximized the matching opportunity because the employee contributed enough to receive the maximum match the company offered. If the employee contributed *more* than 6% of their compensation—say 10%—the employer would still only contribute 3% (50% of the 6% maximum) per the plan. This is because the matching opportunity is limited to 6% of compensation. Conversely, if the employee contributes *less* than 6% of their compensation—say 4%—the employer would contribute only 2%. In this scenario, the match isn't being maximized.

This was the situation in PJ's story. A bright, young professional who is passionate about his job as a real estate analyst, PJ is immersed every day in real estate opportunities and piles of data. Like many, he sometimes needs to pay more attention to the less exciting things about his job, like his 401(k) plan. One day, PJ overhears his colleagues discussing how to maximize their 401(k) match, and he realizes he may be leaving "free money" on the table.

PJ immediately digs in by reading his 401(k) plan's SPD, which summarizes the plan in easy-to-understand language. He reviews the matching formula and realizes that he has been contributing only 4% of his compensation, missing out on the match because his employer matches 50% of contributions up to 6%. PJ immediately changes his election to increase his contribution to 6%. It is tough on his budget, but PJ knows the extra 2% will be matched by an additional 1% from his employer. That is $600 more annually (based on his $60,000 compensation) than he had before, which, over decades, will grow significantly.

This decision is not just about the present; it is about the future, about PJ's dreams of flexibility and wanting to travel and retire early without worrying about his finances. Each dollar contributed today is another step toward that dream. That is the magic of the 401(k) match: It is like a seed, but given time, it can grow into a large tree.

So like PJ, you, too, can make your money work for you. Explore your 401(k) plan thoroughly, understand the matching formula, contribute the maximum amount your budget allows, and make the most of the "free money." Trust me, you will not be sorry.

The two most common matching formulations are partial and full. The partial scenario was illustrated above with PJ's 50% match. In a *fully matched plan*, the employer matches 100% of the employee's contribution, subject to a percentage of compensation limit, often 6%.

For example, if your plan is fully matched with a limit of 6% of compensation, and you contribute 6% of your compensation, your employer will match at a rate of 100% up to 6% of your compensation. That means you contribute 6%, and your employer contributes an additional 6% for 12% total, and you have maximized your match.

If you put in more than 6%, your match will also be maximized, with your employer contributing a maximum of 6%. If, however, you put in *less* than 6% of your compensation, your employer will only match what you put in. So if you put in 4%, the employer matches 100% of that, but it would be only 4%, and you have not fully maximized your match.

As another example, if Louis contributes 4% of his $100,000 salary, he will receive a $4,000 match from his employer, but his maximum match could have been $6,000, so Louis leaves $2,000 on the table.

> **In summary, matching contributions are "free money" because you do not directly pay for them. To get that money, you only must *contribute to yourself*.**

Aim to grab all of your "free money," just like PJ did. This way, you are essentially shopping on Black Friday all year long.

## CONTRIBUTING TOO QUICKLY

It sounds counterintuitive, even ridiculous, but if you contribute too quickly, you can sometimes *lose* a portion of your company's matching contributions. Why would you want to contribute quickly? To invest your contributions as soon as possible, which makes sense to take advantage of the power of compounding as soon as you can. But you need to make sure it is not too fast.

Loss of some portion of a match due to contributing too quickly occurs when you reach your maximum annual contribution limit ($23,000 in 2024 for employees under fifty) before your company completes the match. For example, suppose Lynn elects to contribute 25% of her compensation each bimonthly payroll period. Lynn earns $96,000 annually, or $4,000 each pay period ($96,000 ÷ 24). She contributes $1,000 each pay period to her plan, equal to 25% of compensation ($4,000 × 0.25). The plan provides a 100% match, limited to 6% of compensation, which is $240 per pay period ($4,000 × 0.06).

Lynn may, however, have a problem that should be filed under "no good deed goes unpunished." Although the plan states a contribution limit equal to 25% of compensation, which is $24,000 for Lynn, the Internal Revenue Service (IRS) limits how much she can contribute each year to $23,000. Lynn reaches that limit in the twenty-third pay period by having contributed at the 25% level throughout the year so that she won't have a contribution deducted from her final paycheck of the year.

However, the employer has matched only $5,520 so far over twenty-three pay periods ($240 × 23), and the plan does not make any more matching contributions because, under some plans, when the participant reaches the annual limit before the end of the year, not only do participant contributions stop, but so do the per-payroll matches from your company.

## Optimal Contribution Percentage

You have now determined that contributing too quickly might cause you to lose some matching contributions, which can happen with both pre-tax (traditional) or Roth contributions. Nevertheless, you would like to contribute as soon as possible to grow the money in the market while maximizing the match. What do you do?

The *optimal contribution percentage* helps you get the most out of your contributions and company matches. To do this, you divide the maximum amount that can be contributed yearly ($23,000 in 2024) by your annual compensation. Let's use Lynn as a test case. She has an annual contribution limit of $23,000 and makes $96,000 in yearly compensation. Lynn's optimal contribution percentage is 24% ($23,000 ÷ $96,000), rather than the 25% she had initially elected, which allows her to receive her full 6% match for the year. She can, of course, put in less if she can't afford the maximum contribution, provided she contributes at least 6% to receive the full match. She can also contribute more than 24% but won't get the full match. Her goal is to contribute enough to receive the full match without contributing too much and leaving free matching money on the table.

To apply the formula, you need to determine how the plan defines compensation to calculate contributions, which you can do by referring to your SPD, and you can then review your pay records from the previous year to estimate your current year's compensation, such as base salary and bonus. Then, you can use the optimal contribution percentage to maximize your contributions and match for the year, keeping in mind that the contribution limit can increase yearly. Your plan administrator or a quick search online for the annual 401(k) limit can help you find the limit each year.

## True-Up Matching Contribution

Note that this type of problem can occur only if your company's match is made each pay period or at a different frequency (monthly or quarterly) than once at the end of the year. Some employers make a one-time match at the end of the year, which avoids this issue.

Other companies offer a so-called *true-up matching contribution* designed to ensure that you receive the maximum matching contributions so that you will not have to worry about contributing too quickly to the 401(k) plan. Thus, if you contribute a higher percentage upfront, as Lynn did in the previous example when she contributed 25%, your employer will nevertheless contribute the lost matching money to your account. In Lynn's example, she will receive her "lost" match of $240 if her plan has a true-up feature.

According to the 66th Annual Survey, 67% of 401(k) plans make true-up contributions when the plan does not provide for an annual match, and if that is the case, contributing too quickly is fine. But that means nearly 35% of plans match throughout the year and *do not provide true-ups*. This means that contributing too quickly can be a problem for employees participating in these plans. You should review your plan's SPD to determine whether a true-up applies or contact your plan administrator. A good practice, whenever you contact your plan administrator with questions, is to have them help you find support for their answer in the plan's SPD.

## OTHER MATCHING OPPORTUNITIES (AND LIMITATIONS)

Several other things can affect whether or not your match is maximized.

*Automatic enrollment:* If your plan automatically enrolls you at a lower contribution percentage than needed to receive the employer's maximum match, consider raising your contribution to the required level if you can afford to do so.

*Vesting:* Keep an eye on your vesting date—the date that contributions are yours to keep and cannot be forfeited. (See chapter 18 for more information.) You may lose some or all your matching contributions if you leave your job before becoming vested.

*The Roth match:* Some plans allow employees to receive a portion or all of their matching contributions on a Roth basis. Employees who are early in their careers and have a low tax rate may want to consider this option. This means the money you receive as a match will be taxed now but not later when you take it out. (See chapter 6 for more information.) It is up to the employer to decide whether to offer this option, and this is another instance where you should refer to your SPD and contact the plan administrator if you need clarification on whether your employer provides Roth 401(k) matches and how it works. Note that you must specifically elect this if you decide to take advantage of the Roth match. Also, if a Roth match is not available now, it might become an option in the future, so stay alert for updates to your benefits package.

*Matching contributions on student debt:* Historically, employers were permitted to make matching contributions based only on an employee's 401(k) plan contributions. But this meant some employees, especially at the beginning of their careers, were missing out on their employer-matching contributions and losing significant growth in their long-term retirement savings because high student debt precluded them from making contributions. This problem was addressed in legislation commonly known as SECURE 2.0. Now, employers may choose to make matching contributions to 401(k) plans based on the employee's student loan payments, even if the employee doesn't contribute to the plan. If your employer offers this opportunity, you will simply need to certify that you've made your student loan payments annually in lieu of the contributions.

# SUMMARY

- Your employer's 401(k) match is free money. Your goal should be to maximize the match by contributing enough to receive the total allowable match for the year.
- If you contribute too quickly, you risk losing a portion of the matching contribution unless your plan provides a true-up or a one-time match at year-end. However, you can mitigate this loss by calculating your optimal contribution percentage.
- Other opportunities and restrictions to keep in mind are automatic enrollment features, the vesting schedule, Roth matching options, and student debts as a basis for your matches.

# CHAPTER 8

## Opportunity Five—Turbocharge with Catch-Up Contributions

401(k) participants who are fifty or over get another opportunity to secure their financial future by taking advantage of a feature available in many plans called the *catch-up contribution*. (Younger workers may want to alert their working parents to this commonly overlooked 401(k) feature as well.) The basic deal is this: If you are fifty or older, you can save even more money in your retirement plan through catch-up contributions. It is like giving your savings a turbocharge! Whether or not you have been a diligent saver, catch-up contributions make sense to take advantage of if they are affordable.

Let's meet Lisa, who took full advantage of a second-chance opportunity. When she was younger, Lisa focused solely on her career and did not pay much attention to her health and fitness. She barely worked out and ate too much junk food. Lisa started to feel increasingly worse as she aged. She was constantly tired, put on weight, and faced more and more health issues. She was upset that she hadn't taken better care of herself when she was younger.

Lisa decided to get serious about her health at age fifty-two. She joined a nearby gym that offered specialized programs, like personalized workout plans and advice on what to eat. She worked on getting in shape and even learned how to play tennis and pickleball. Thankful for the second chance to do these things before dealing with a major emergency, she saw her health improve over time and felt better than she had in years. She especially loved her new life once she figured out how to keep score in pickleball.

People fortunate enough to get a second chance should try to take full advantage of this opportunity. For Lisa, it meant getting her health back on track. For others, it can mean taking advantage of the catch-up contribution opportunity.

> **Older employees enrolled in 401(k) plans get a second chance to enhance their financial security by making catch-up contributions once they reach age fifty.**

## CATCH-UP CONTRIBUTIONS: BACKGROUND

These features, which allow individuals aged fifty and over to increase contributions to their 401(k) plans as retirement draws nearer, were enacted into law because Congress was concerned that people approaching retirement had not saved enough. Surprisingly, despite the availability of catch-up features in almost all 401(k) plans, only 32% of participants take advantage of this opportunity.[1] Your specific plan may allow catch-ups as traditional contributions (before tax), Roth contributions (after tax), or a combination. But you need to take action to make this happen.

Fortunately, as you progress in age and career, your income generally increases, making catch-up contributions especially practical. Whether you have been a diligent saver or started planning for retirement later in your career, you can take advantage of this opportunity to add more to your 401(k) plan. In 2024, the catch-up feature allowed for an additional $7,500 per year on top of the regular contribution limit of $23,000. Keep in mind that these limits are adjusted annually to account for inflation.

## THE POWER OF THE CATCH-UP

Let me share a story about my friend Jason. After winning a tennis match against me (yes, I am a good sport about it!), Jason and I sat down for coffee and discussed retirement. He was turning fifty at the time and was worried that he had not saved enough. He had about $490,000 in his 401(k) account, to which he had contributed since he was twenty-five at $5,000 per year. Jason had made total contributions of $125,000 ($5,000 × 25 years) by then and accumulated gains of $365,000 (the current value of $490,000 – the $125,000 he had contributed). He could have contributed even more over the years if he had paid closer attention to his savings, but he hadn't.

Jason's current annual income was now $90,000, and I advised him to increase his regular contributions to the maximum allowable percentage in his plan of 15% of compensation ($13,500 per year) *and* add $7,500 through catch-up contributions (for a total of $21,000 per year). This could accumulate approximately $2,700,000 by the time he reached sixty-five, assuming a 10% annual return. Moreover, this calculation does not even include any company-matching contributions. On the other hand, if Jason failed to increase his contributions, his accumulations at age sixty-five would be around 26% lower, totaling about $2,200,000—a $500,000 difference.

Of course, not everyone can afford such a significant contribution jump, but if you can, go for it! And even if you contribute less than the maximum $7,500 catch-up amount, you can still make a significant difference in your financial security during retirement. By age fifty, you are typically more established financially and likely more able to save a little more. It may feel too late, but as Yogi Berra, the iconic Yankee catcher, famously said, "It ain't over till it's over." You can make the election and change the amount at any time. Contact your plan administrator or access your account online to make these extra contributions.

## CATCH-UP LIMITATIONS

Everything comes with a restriction or limit it seems. In the case of the catch-up contribution, you can make this contribution only after you've reached your plan's contribution limit, which is either the maximum contribution percentage limit or the annual dollar limit ($23,000 in 2024). Let us explore some examples to clarify.

*Maximum contribution percentage limit:* Bethany is over fifty, earns $50,000, and contributes 12% of her salary to her retirement plan, the maximum contribution percentage according to her SPD. Since her plan allows catch-up contributions, she is eligible to make them, given that she contributes at the maximum contribution percentage of 12% and is over age fifty. Her regular contributions amount to $6,000 per year (0.12 × $50,000), and with the catch-up contributions, she can contribute an additional $7,500 for a total of $13,500.

*Annual dollar limit:* Willie is also over fifty years old and earns $120,000. He decided to contribute 20% of his salary to his retirement plan, even though the plan has a 30% cap. Willie has been limited to $23,000 and is prohibited from contributing the full $24,000 (0.2 × $120,000) due to the annual dollar limit. However, Willie can now make catch-up contributions because he is fifty years old and reached the $23,000 annual dollar limit. As a result, he can make a full $7,500 catch-up contribution in addition to his $23,000 for a total contribution of $30,500 for the year.

## OTHER CONSIDERATIONS

*Matching the catch-up:* According to the 66th Annual Survey, nearly 64% of plans match catch-up contributions, and your plan's SPD will indicate if yours does.[2] However, there may be caps that limit or eliminate the matching amount, so it is crucial to understand how the catch-up-related match works in your situation. Of course, if your catch-up contributions are matched, they become even more valuable!

*Increased contribution limit for older participants:* Beginning in 2025, eligible participants who attain ages sixty, sixty-one, sixty-two, or sixty-three (but not age sixty-four) during the year will be able to make even larger catch-up contributions, equal to the greater of $10,000 or 150% of the age fifty catch-up limit in effect for 2025. This change will allow participants very close to retirement to save even more through their 401(k) plans.

*Highly paid 401(k) plan participants:* Beginning in 2026, catch-up contributions must be made as Roth contributions for plan participants earning over $145,000 (adjusted yearly) in the previous calendar year. This means the catch-up will be immediately taxable. It would be best to look out for notices from your plan to determine how much to balance your overall contributions between Roth and traditional accounts. For example, some highly paid 401(k) plan participants may decide that their non-catch-up contributions will be traditional due to their high earnings and tax bracket, given that they will also contribute to a Roth account with their catch-ups.

## SUMMARY

- Catch-ups allow participants aged fifty and over to increase their contributions to 401(k) plans as they get closer to retirement.
- Making these additional contributions is like turbocharging your retirement savings.
- Plan limitations may impact how much you can contribute as a catch-up adjustment.
- Other catch-up considerations include matching terms, increased opportunity for older adults, and restrictions on highly paid employees.

# CHAPTER 9

## Opportunity Six—Refer to Key Documents When in Doubt

Peter, a new employee working three days a week, decides it's time to get serious about his future and calls his new company's 401(k) support line. With a confident smile, he asks the representative, "When can I enroll in the 401(k) plan?"

The representative, juggling phone calls and coffee, quickly checks and says, "Oh, you're part-time? Sorry, you can't enroll in the 401(k) plan." Peter, trusting the advice, doesn't enroll. After all, the support line rep should know. Right?

It turns out that Peter's 401(k) plan document and related SPD state that part-time employees like Peter *are* eligible to enroll! Oops, the rep made a mistake, and Peter lost money. Peter could have promptly corrected this error by cross-checking this advice against the plan's SPD. I suggest you ask the plan representatives to review the specific SPD language with you whenever you pose questions so you can understand their advice and make sure it makes sense.

This type of error is common, and I have seen it occur more often during my career than you might think. Just like in the game of telephone, where messages get hilariously garbled, getting crucial advice from a support representative, who checks with another source, can lead to misunderstandings—although these are not funny! I have seen many other company mistakes, such as inadequate contributions and failure to follow participant instructions (see part 3 for more examples).

> **Costly errors can be promptly corrected or mitigated when participants review key plan documents, notices, and account statements.**

This chapter will introduce you to the most important documents that will help you understand your plan and optimize your participation. I suggest you obtain and file these documents so you can easily reference them. These documents can be provided on paper or furnished electronically. Participants have a right to request paper copies or opt out of electronic delivery.

## SUMMARY PLAN DESCRIPTION

The SPD is one of the most important documents you will receive upon participating in a 401(k) or profit-sharing plan. Pension plans are also required to provide this document. An SPD must generally be provided to each participant and beneficiary within ninety days of enrollment. The SPD describes your benefits, rights, and obligations in easy-to-understand language and must legally contain certain essential information. As the name suggests, it summarizes the more detailed and technical plan document.

If you have questions about your plan, you should start by referring to the SPD, which is often prepared by an outside law firm, consulting firm, or brokerage firm like Fidelity. If you have trouble finding the information in the SPD, you can often locate an appropriate contact through your plan's portal. You can also contact your human resources department to ask for help or for a referral to someone who can. Many plans keep the SPDs online for easy access. Make sure you have this document. If not, request it in writing.

My wife and I have been 401(k) participants for decades and constantly refer to the SPD when we have questions, most of which can be quickly answered.

## SUMMARY OF MATERIAL MODIFICATIONS

If any significant feature of your plan changes, you will (or should) re-ceive a summary of material modifications (SMM). Significant features include the matching contribution formula and a description of eli-gible participants (e.g., full-time and part-time employees). A revised SPD can be provided instead of the SMM. Whichever document you receive must explain plan changes and be easy to understand. Your plan administrator must provide the SMM (or revised SPD) within 210 days (seven months) after the end of the year in which the change is adopted. There is a good chance you will receive notice of a major plan change in advance, including changes in the law, intended to give you time to respond, if necessary or desired.

Whenever you receive an SMM, pay close attention so you can act quickly and react appropriately if necessary. For example, if the com-pany's matching formula changes, you might want to adjust your con-tribution allocation. When you snooze, you sometimes lose.

## PLAN DOCUMENT

The plan document contains all plan provisions in detailed, technical terms instead of the "plain English" words in the SPD. This includes information regarding eligibility, vesting, distributions, investments, and more. This is the primary document that governs your rights and obligations under the plan. This document is not provided automat-ically, but administrators must provide it upon request. You should always first refer to the plan's SPD as it is far simpler and easier to un-derstand, and you can do only your best with your limited time.

Occasionally, your employer might change or amend the plan doc-ument; if that happens, you will receive an SMM (or revised SPD) to inform you of the change.

## FEE DISCLOSURE

401(k) plans are required to provide fee and expense explanations to participants.[1] This includes plan-related information and investment-related information. This information, required by the US Department of Labor, ensures that workers have the information they need to make informed investment decisions. Fees are important to consider because they may significantly reduce your account's growth and your retirement income, making it important to know about the different types of fees and the ways in which they are charged.

Plan-related information must be provided to participants before they can direct their investments and annually thereafter. The information falls into several categories:

*General plan information:* Refers to the plan's structure and mechanics, such as how to give investment instructions, a current list of investment options under the plan, and a list of arrangements that enable the selection of investments other than those designated by the plan, such as brokerage windows (an optional feature that allows participants to invest in a wide variety of investments beyond the core options offered by the plan).

*Plan administration fees:* The plan pays these fees to the party responsible for the task. For example, it is common for companies to hire third parties, such as Schwab or ADP, to manage portions of their plans, and these fees are paid to them. The document describes fees and expenses for the daily operation of plan services, such as legal, accounting, recordkeeping, and trustee services. Plans often offer other services, such as customer service representatives, telephone voice response systems, and online transactions. Sometimes, these fees are paid by your company or charged against the plan assets. If paid by the plan, these fees can be deducted from or charged to all participant accounts.

*Investment fees:* This is the largest category of fees by a wide margin. These fees are paid as an indirect deduction to your account since they are charged directly from your investment returns. These fees are important to monitor. They are usually stated as a percentage of the amount of assets in the fund. For example, a participant has invested over the years and has saved $200,000 in his account. If his expense ratio is 1% yearly, his annual fee is $2,000. For investment options with a fixed rate of return, any shareholder fees or restrictions on the participant's ability to purchase or withdraw from the investment must be provided. This data enables the participant to determine how much the investment option costs.

*Individual service fees:* Individual service fees for optional features under a 401(k) plan may also be charged directly to individual participant accounts based on the account owner's actions, such as taking out plan loans.

*Investment-related information:* This must also be included in the fee disclosure and contains several subcategories.

*Performance data:* Specific historical investment performances, with one-, five-, and ten-year returns, are disclosed for investment options, such as mutual funds, that do not have fixed rates of return. This data also includes the annual rate of return and the investment term for investment options that do have a fixed or stated return (e.g., fixed interest rate for a stated period or term).

*Benchmark information:* This includes the name and returns of a securities market index over one-, five-, and ten-year periods for investment options without a fixed rate of return. (Investment options with fixed rates of return are not subject to this disclosure requirement.)

Other information covered in the fee disclosure section of the plan document include the plan's website address, a glossary of terms, and investment-related fees that might apply outside the fund's expense ratio, such as sales charges, commonly referred to as loads, that investors pay when they buy or sell shares in a mutual fund. (Many mutual funds do not charge sales fees, and some plans deduct your share of these fees from your accounts.)

## PARTICIPANT STATEMENTS

All 401(k) plans that permit participants to direct their investments, which most do, must automatically provide statements at least quarterly. These statements provide important information about the benefits you have earned. Plans that do not allow participant direction (as with a small number of profit-sharing plans) must provide annual statements to participants.

Individual account plans, including 401(k) plans, must also add a lifetime income explanation to at least one statement during each twelve-month period. This shows a simplified estimate of how the current account balance might be distributed as monthly income payments over the account owner's life and over the joint life of the account owner and their spouse. While the projections are based on standard assumptions that can change over time, they can serve as a helpful foundation for participants to evaluate how well they are doing in terms of saving for retirement.

I briefly review my statements quarterly to ensure they look reasonable. I don't focus on the size of the gains or losses, as I am in it for the long term—although, sometimes, I need an aspirin or even a drink.

## OTHER IMPORTANT NOTICES AND STATEMENTS

In addition to the documents described, you will periodically receive various notices and statements. Although they might feel cumbersome and technical to read, they contain important information you need to understand.

*Investment fund mapping notice:* These notices explain how assets will be mapped, or reallocated, if a fund is eliminated from your plan. A fund may be dropped for many reasons, including high fees, low returns, or change in management. Participants who had assets in the eliminated fund and did not select an alternative fund offered by the plan will see those assets reinvested in the newly mapped fund. The mapping notice contains information regarding the existing fund and new investment options, and administrators must provide at least thirty days' notice about the changes (and not more than sixty days).

Be on the lookout for these mapping notices and pay close attention to understand where your assets will be reinvested. If you believe an alternate fund offered by your plan better suits your needs, be sure to select the alternative. When reviewing the existing fund and the proposed replacement, consider the same types of factors you assessed when making your initial selections, such as the fund's performance, risk, and expense ratio, and compare this information with other available offerings.

*Blackout notice:* A notice must be sent out to participants to notify them of a blackout lasting three business days or more. When blackouts are imposed, participants cannot direct or diversify their accounts, obtain loans, or take distributions. Corporate mergers and acquisitions and changes in the investment lineup or recordkeepers are the most common reasons for a blackout period. The blackout notice will tell you the expected beginning and end dates of the blackout period and what rights are being restricted during that timeframe. Administrators must provide this notice at least thirty days (and at most sixty days) before the blackout. If you receive one, pay attention so that you can make time-sensitive account adjustments, such as changing an investment, obtaining a loan, or taking a distribution, if needed, before being blocked during the blackout.

*Safe harbor 401(k) plans:* These plans must meet several minimum requirements, such as containing employer contributions that are 100% immediately vested. Including these requirements allows the plan to avoid the need for complicated testing and administration. These contributions can be matching or nonelective. Participants are notified about their rights and obligations thirty to ninety days before each plan year. Participants who have these plans are fortunate and should try to take advantage of their generous contributions and immediate vesting.

*Qualified default investment alternative (QDIA) notice:* This notice provides information about a plan's qualified default investment alternatives (QDIAs) for employees who do not make proactive decisions. Under automatic enrollment features, for example, most employees will take no action and become enrolled in the plan by default. If that happens, the contribution is directed to the QDIA. The QDIA notice, which must be provided at least thirty days before the participant's eligibility, explains the QDIA feature and the employee's ability to transfer all or part of the QDIA investment to any other alternative under the plan and the QDIA expense ratio. The plan administrator must also provide an annual statement at least thirty days before each plan year. A target date fund is a common QDIA. These funds automatically adjust their mix of stocks, bonds, and so forth to become more conservative as time passes.

If your account is invested in a QDIA, you might want to transfer it to a different fund that better meets your needs. For example, the fees might be too high or the fund's investment mix too conservative for your situation. The QDIA notice will describe how to make these changes.

*Notices for automatic enrollment:* Under an automatic enrollment plan, an employee is deemed to have elected to contribute a percentage of compensation to the plan unless the employee elects in writing to decline participation. In other words, the plan does not require employees to opt *in* to participate; instead, it allows them to opt *out*. There are several types of automatic enrollment plans, and they generally require that a notice describing each employee's rights and obligations be given to each participant within a reasonable time before each plan year. Such a notice can be combined with the QDIA notice described above.

If you are automatically enrolled in a plan, ensure your participation level and the investments are appropriate. If they are not, adjust them. Please do not rely on the automatic levels because they may not suit your retirement needs. For example, the automatic contribution may be too high or too low for your current situation, it might not satisfactorily help you achieve your financial goals in retirement, or it might fail to maximize your matching benefits. If changes need to be made, the automatic enrollment notice will describe how and when this needs to be done.

## SUMMARY

- **The plan document is the primary governing document that contains all key information about your 401(k) plan.**
- **Because the plan document can be cumbersome and difficult to read, the key document that you should become most familiar with is your SPD. Always cross-check critical advice from your employer or plan administrator against the SPD to mitigate errors and maximize your participation and benefits.**
- **Multiple important notices and statements are also provided to participants. Be sure to pay regular attention especially to the participant statements and the fee disclosure notice.**

# CHAPTER 10

## Opportunity Seven—What to Do with Your Retirement Assets After You Leave

Retirement or career changes can be exciting times. But your trusted 401(k) needs some attention whenever you step away from your current job. The options, such as rolling over your funds to a new plan, transferring it to an IRA, or leaving it with your prior plan may appear to be straightforward, but each option has pros and cons that need to be considered so your retirement account is transitioned appropriately.

A related 401(k) issue that sometimes crops up when changing jobs is declining 401(k) savings rates. Reasons for this include forgetting to enroll in the new plan or enrolling automatically at the new plan's default rate, which is lower than the contribution rate under the prior plan. Your new 401(k) election should be considered, even before looking at your prior account transition options.

According to a recent study from Vanguard, declining savings rates after job changes can cost a participant $300,000 over forty years, assuming a starting salary of $60,000.[1] Vanguard found that a typical employee changes jobs eight times during their career. And each move results in an increase of 10% in salary yet a decrease of 0.7% in the 401(k) savings rate. This decline was found to eliminate approximately six years of retirement spending. Be mindful of this when transitioning to a new employer, and do your best to remember to increase, or at least maintain, your savings rate, particularly if you are fortunate enough to get a raise.

Interestingly, another Vanguard study highlights a different problem related to changing jobs. Here, the study involves liquidating a 401(k) after changing jobs, rolling it to an IRA, and unintentionally leaving the IRA in cash for many years, causing a significant loss in investment returns. The account owner sometimes does not reinvest because they are used to automatic investment and believe the funds will be automatically invested when they switch jobs.

The Vanguard study found that 28% of those who rolled savings into IRAs in 2015 still had their money in cash seven years later. Vanguard estimates an aggregate annual benefit to all rollover investors of over $170 billion in potential asset growth if all uninvested cash were to be invested in the market.[2] This is a vast problem.

Before we discuss reinvesting your funds, the first step is to decide what to do with your retirement assets. There are five possible choices about how to handle your retirement assets: Leave them where they are, transfer them to your new employer's 401(k), roll them into an IRA, cash out, or convert them into a Roth IRA. Several crucial factors need to be considered before deciding which route to take.

## CRUCIAL FACTORS TO THINK ABOUT

*Consolidation and management ease:* Consolidating your accounts under one plan administrator means combining multiple accounts into one plan. This can streamline your financial management. The process keeps everything under one roof, making your financial life less chaotic. For example, one login (and one login password), not several, makes it easier to jump online and view or make changes to your portfolio.

*Fees:* Understanding and reviewing the fees associated with your options is also key. Lower fees benefit your savings growth because fees reduce your assets and returns. This is especially important when comparing 401(k) plans to IRAs, as many 401(k) plans, particularly larger ones, have lower fees (expense ratios) than the funds offered by

IRA providers. Be sure to compare the expense ratios of your various investment options, as these fees are often the most significant component of costs.

*Investment flexibility:* IRA holders can choose from a wide variety of investment options, often choosing from thousands of options, whereas the *employer* generally selects investment choices in a typical 401(k) plan, limiting them to about twenty options. In my experience, however, 401(k) investment offerings provide the diversity needed to meet most individual goals. More is not always better.

*Asset protection:* 401(k) plans may offer greater protection against creditors than IRAs. Generally, creditors or others cannot seize 401(k) accounts, with a few exceptions, including divorce and the IRS. Thus, they offer a very high level of security. ERISA, a US law that requires safeguards in most 401(k) plans in the private sector, requires that plan funds be protected so participants receive their benefits.

On the other hand, IRAs are not subject to ERISA; therefore, they do not always provide the same amount of security.[3] IRAs protect up to about $1.5 million in bankruptcy, but outside of bankruptcy, your protection level ultimately depends on state law.[4] If, for example, you get into a car accident and judgment is rendered against you for damages, your IRA could be taken to satisfy the judgment, depending on the protection afforded to IRAs by your state. Most states provide some level of security, but the safest and easiest asset protection approach is a 401(k) plan, which will always be protected from creditors, period. There is no need to check state law for the answer or rely on the advice given.

Indeed, my wife and I have left our 401(k)s at prior employers, in part, for this reason. It is easier not to deal with state law, which is also subject to change at any time. We also kept the funds in our previous plans because they had better and lower-cost investment options. If you decide to roll over assets to your IRA and are at high risk for litigation (such as if you are a doctor), you should review this with your advisor, as it can be complicated.

## WHAT ARE YOUR ALTERNATIVES?

Let's look closer at your five options for managing your hard-earned retirement funds as you move from one employer to another.

*Option 1—Leave your funds behind in your prior employer's plan:* This entails managing multiple accounts and is, as a result, more difficult than a combined approach. On the other hand, you don't have to take action. Also, fees can sometimes be lower and investment options better in your prior plan.

*My recommendation:* It depends! If the new plan lacks quality index funds with low fees, leave your old plan intact. But if the investment lineup is subpar in your prior employer's plan, transfer your account to your new employer's plan.

*Option 2—Roll over your old account to your new employer's plan:* Here, your new and old assets are combined under one plan, which makes managing them far easier. Hopefully, the new plan will offer similar or even better investment options, although there is a risk that it won't.

*My recommendation:* Consider this option if the new plan offers several quality index funds with low fees so that you can consolidate your retirement assets and simplify your financial life.

*Option 3—Roll over from your old account to an IRA:* This option offers a much more extensive range of investment choices than an employer plan. However, it can result in the loss of important legal protections that 401(k) plans offer.

*My recommendation:* Roll over to an IRA if your investment options in your prior and new plans are subpar.

*Option 4—Cash out:* This provides immediate funds, which could be important, particularly in emergencies. However, this comes with major downsides, including taxes, if you are withdrawing from a traditional 401(k), and it could also mean substantial penalties if you are withdrawing from any retirement account before age fifty-nine and a half. And depending on how you manage the cash, it could also mean the loss of future growth potential.

This is *not generally recommended* before you retire.

*Option 5—Convert your traditional 401(k) funds to a Roth IRA:* This allows for future tax-free growth, but it comes with immediate tax liability as you will need to pay taxes on all the contributions, matches, and subsequent investment earnings at the time of conversion. If the amount converted is large, your current tax bill can significantly increase.

*My recommendation:* Consider this option if you expect to be in a low tax bracket during the year you would convert, such as if your income declines significantly after losing a job or making a major career change.

> **While each option has its benefits and drawbacks, you should generally try to leave your retirement funds in whatever 401(k) or IRA plan offers the best investment options, and possibly asset protection, with the highest returns and lowest fees.**

## TWO GOOD ROLLOVER OPTIONS

Looking on the brighter side, the good news about options 2 and 3 above is that rolling over your 401(k) to an IRA or to your new employer's 401(k) lets your money continue to grow and compound without tax implications. Tax payments remain deferred when you roll over your retirement assets until you withdraw them later. By rolling over, you are saving for your future, and your money continues to grow tax-deferred (or tax-free if it is a Roth).

A rollover can be handled in one of three ways, but only two are recommended:

*Direct rollover—401(k):* Your previous 401(k) plan administrator sends the money directly to your new plan or IRA. Your plan may issue your distribution as a check payable to your new account, but no taxes will be withheld from your transfer. This applies only to a 401(k) plan distribution, not an IRA.

*Trustee-to-trustee transfer—IRA:* Your financial firm moves the money from your IRA to another IRA or retirement plan. You will need to contact your IRA custodian for instructions. Taxes are not withheld. This option applies to distributions from an IRA, not from a 401(k) plan.

## THE ROLLOVER TRANSACTION TO AVOID

The third way to roll over your money is with the *sixty-day rollover*. In this scenario, you receive a check payable to you and have sixty days to deposit it into the new 401(k) plan or IRA. But if you miss the deadline, you will be taxed. It is just like a high-stakes game of beat-the-clock. In rare cases, the sixty-day deadline can be waived by the IRS, but it is generally strictly enforced.

Let's discuss why the sixty-day rollover option should not be used. First, the direct rollover and trustee-to-trustee transfer options are easier to understand and less likely to go wrong. I have witnessed numerous problems with sixty-day rollovers, such as lost checks and missed deadlines, which led to significant taxes.

Marjorie, a retiree, had substantial funds in multiple IRA bank accounts. She kept most of her funds in cash certificates of deposit (CDs) for safety when interest rates were attractive, allowing her to receive an acceptable return. When a CD matured, she would look for a new bank with a better rate. Late on a Friday morning, Marjorie called me in a frenzy. "I lost my $50,000 IRA check," she said, almost in tears. "I think I left it in one of the magazines I read at the beauty parlor. I may have used it as a bookmark." You can imagine her panic!

You might think this was no big deal. Couldn't she have had the check canceled and asked for a new one to be issued? The answer is *not necessarily*. This is not so easy because receiving a replacement bank check can take ninety days or more. Marjorie did call her bank to request a replacement check, but as it turned out she found the check a week later in a filing cabinet, where she had filed it for "safekeeping." Many are less fortunate than Marjorie and forget to take care of the check and roll over the funds within the deadline. These situations can result in taxes and penalties, which is an expensive lesson. Note that this problem applies only if the check is made out in Marjorie's name, not if it's issued to the IRA or plan for her benefit.

Another reason to avoid the sixty-day rollover relates to cash flow. Whenever a 401(k) distribution is made, a mandatory 20% tax is withheld, and it can take some time to get that back. But you need to deposit the full amount of the distribution into your new 401(k) within sixty days to avoid the taxes and penalties. (There is also a 20% withholding for IRAs unless you choose to have a different amount withheld or opt out of withholding.)

James, who is forty-seven years old, received a $25,000 distribution from his 401(k) plan when he changed jobs. His former employer withheld $5,000 (0.20 × $25,000) from the distribution, so his net distribution was $20,000. But James still needed to deposit the entire $25,000 in his new plan account in order for it to qualify as a rollover. Unfortunately, James did not have the extra $5,000 available. As a result, he could roll over only $20,000 and was taxed on the additional $5,000 that he couldn't roll over because of the mandatory withholding. Additionally, a 10% penalty tax was applied to him for withdrawing the $5,000 before he was fifty-nine and a half. It was a costly lesson for James. Ouch!

Yet a third reason to avoid the sixty-day rollover option is that there is a limit to how many sixty-day IRA rollovers you can do within twelve months: *just one*, regardless of the number of IRAs you own. Keeping track of this can be challenging, lead to errors, and result in significant tax consequences. The one-per-year limit does not apply to 401(k) or other plans, IRA rollovers to 401(k) plans, or IRA conversions (traditional to Roth).[5]

Lastly, it is crucial to note that certain payments, like required minimum distributions, cannot be rolled over.

For more information on Roth conversions, see chapter 6 for a discussion of in-plan conversions and chapter 14 for a discussion of IRA conversions. Rollovers of company stock have some additional considerations and are covered in chapter 11.

## WHY CASHING OUT IS A PROBLEM

The bad news: Withdrawals from 401(k)s are taxed. This means you should cash out your 401(k) early only if you enjoy paying taxes and penalties. This has already been stated, but it bears repeating because many people don't realize the severe taxes and penalties for cashing out a 401(k) early: ordinary income taxes on the withdrawal for any reason as well as a potential 10% penalty tax if you are not yet fifty-nine and a half years old. Of course, the IRS loves it when you cash out early because it considers the heavy tax burden you suffer as its "revenue." It cannot wait to get its paws on your cash! State income taxes may also apply, depending on where you live. Let's look at a quick example.

Gigi was thirty-eight when she left her job at IBM with $100,000 in her 401(k) account. She was in an average 20% federal and 5% state tax bracket, and she chose to cash out. But that account balance was viewed as income by the tax authorities, and her choice bumped her federal and state brackets up to 22% and 6%, respectively, because the tax rates increase as income increases. On top of that, Gigi also got smacked with a 10% early withdrawal penalty because of her age. Ultimately, Gigi paid 38% in taxes, or $38,000, which she wouldn't have had to do if she'd rolled over her retirement funds. You can see why the IRS is celebrating.

With few exceptions, therefore, a rollover is a far better choice than cashing out when you leave your job. Also, in some instances, small balances of less than $5,000 may be cashed out by the plan automatically, but they can still ultimately be rolled over. See your plan's summary for details.

## SUMMARY

- **Whenever you leave your job, you need to proactively decide what to do with your retirement funds. Things to consider when making this choice include consolidation and management ease, fees, investment flexibility, and asset protection.**
- **Options include keeping your funds with your previous employer's plan, rolling over to the new employer's plan, rolling over to an IRA, cashing out, or converting from a traditional retirement asset to a Roth asset.**
- **The cash-out option should also be avoided due to taxes, penalties, and loss of future growth potential.**
- **When rolling over, avoid the sixty-day rollover trap. It's generally better to opt for a direct rollover or a trustee-to-trustee transfer.**

# CHAPTER 11

## Opportunity Eight—Navigate Company Stock with Care

Amy, a colleague, shared this story with me. She was juggling multiple meetings with no time for a break. In the middle of her day, a distressed coworker told her that her company stock was crashing and that the attorney general was investigating. The news spread quickly through the company, and her colleagues were able to sell company stock at a small loss before it crashed further. But Amy was stuck in meetings and missed out on the ability to sell during the day. By the end of the day, it was too late. Her stock had dropped significantly, leaving her in a scary financial situation without any good options.

Those who invest in company stock put all their eggs in one basket—their livelihood and retirement savings are tied to their company's financial future. Problems at their company might cause declines in the stock price and reductions in their compensation or even the loss of their job. Because this means that both your investments and compensation depend on the same company, this level of risk is generally not recommended for 401(k) participants. Morningstar's head of retirement research, David Blanchett, said that the ideal allocation to employer securities, from a research perspective, is *zero* due to the above concerns, although he also noted that this zero limit on total portfolio assets for company stock ownership might not be practical and that 10% of total assets is a reasonable upper limit.[1] Generally, the sooner you can diversify, the better. Blanchett also found that participants who have allocated high aggregate allocations to company stock have generally underperformed those who don't.

> **The appeal of company stock can be deceiving; it may look like an opportunity, but it often isn't and should be approached cautiously.**

## WHY DIVERSIFY

*Company stock*, also referred to as *employer securities*, is an investment in your employer's business. Some companies offer this investment within their 401(k) plans—and some provide matching contributions exclusively in the form of their stock. Others present it as an option among several funds, allowing you to make an informed choice. Offering company stock can help align participants' interests with the company's.

But participants in defined contribution plans—such as 401(k) and profit-sharing plans, except certain employee stock ownership plans—must have *the right to divest* employer securities in their accounts and reinvest in several diversified investment options. The plan must give participants notice of their diversification rights no later than thirty days before the first date a participant can exercise their diversification rights. The notice must describe not only the diversification rights but also the importance of diversifying retirement plan investment.

Suppose company stock is offered as an investment in your 401(k) plan for your contributions, including employee after-tax and rollover contributions. In that case, investing is voluntary—you can choose to invest. If the employer match or profit-sharing contribution is offered *only* in company stock, you may be able to immediately diversify by transferring the value of that investment to one of the plan's other investment options. However, sometimes, your rights to diversify can be somewhat restricted.

In some 401(k) plans, you must wait to move the company stock, initially contributed as a company match or profit-sharing contribution, until you have been with the company for three years. In this type of plan, the participants must be offered at least three investment options other than company stock. And some employee stock ownership plans may have no diversification rights or longer waiting periods than three years. Review your SPD to check if your plan offers company stock and what diversification rules apply.

## WHAT HAPPENS ON TERMINATION

The previous chapter explored how to handle retirement assets other than company stock when you leave your employer. Now, let us explore distributions of company stock held by your retirement account. Normally, when leaving a company, rolling over your entire account is often the best choice. But that may not be the case for holdings of company stock. When rolled over into a traditional IRA, it will not be taxed at the time of rollover, but it will be taxed based on the account's *value*, at ordinary income tax rates, when withdrawn during retirement. Depending on your tax bracket, this can lead to taxes as high as 30% to 40% (or even more) of the distribution and can be particularly costly if the value of the company's stock rises over time.

An alternative strategy is to move the company stock into a taxable account, such as a nonretirement brokerage account, when you change jobs. When you do this, you will be taxed on the *cost* of the stock when it was contributed to your account, rather than its current appreciated value at the time of the withdrawal. At the time you sell the stock years later, the *appreciation* will be taxed at *long-term capital gains* rates, which are typically lower than ordinary income tax rates. You can obtain the cost basis information from your employer.

To illustrate, let us consider Fred's story. After investing in Merck stock for two decades at an average price of $10 per share, Fred leaves the company for another opportunity. At the time of his departure, each of his thousand shares is worth $100, for a total account value of $100,000. Fred has two options.

Under option 1, Fred moves the stock to a taxable, nonretirement account and pays tax based on the cost of the stock ($10 per share) because he is taking it out of a retirement fund. His tax basis is a total of $10,000, so in this case, Fred is taxed on only the $10,000. Assuming a 35% ordinary income tax bracket, his tax amounts to $3,500. Of course, he would also be subject to a 10% early withdrawal tax of $1,000 (0.10 × $10,000) if the withdrawal occurs before age fifty-nine and a half, resulting in a total tax of $4,500. With this option, Fred waits to sell the stock until he eventually retires from the second company many years later when its value has increased to $150,000. At that point, he will pay taxes on the appreciation of $140,000 ($150,000 fair market value – the $10,000 cost basis) at the capital gains rates of either 15% or 20%, depending on his income. Assuming a 20% capital gains rate, his tax on the appreciation would amount to $28,000 ($140,000 × 0.20). Therefore, Fred's total tax would be $32,500 ($28,000 + the original $4,500 tax and penalty).

Under option 2, Fred rolls over his account into an IRA when he leaves Merck and pays no taxes at the time. But he will pay taxes later, at retirement, when he withdraws the funds. Assuming Fred withdraws the total account balance of $150,000 at retirement as a lump sum, he will have to pay taxes at an assumed ordinary income tax rate of 35%. This results in a total tax bill of $52,500 (150,000 × 35%).

By choosing option 1, Fred paid only $32,500 in taxes and saved $20,000 ($52,500 – $32,500). Comparing the two options, it becomes clear that option 1 offers significant tax savings for Fred because he was able to take advantage of being taxed on the low-cost basis of his stock and lower capital gains rates on the gain in years later.

It is important to note that this strategy is complex and requires a *total account distribution* when you leave the employer. The stock is distributed "in kind," but any other assets included in the account can be rolled over. This strategy may benefit those who own highly appreciated stock in their plan and anticipate being in a high tax bracket when selling it.

## SUMMARY

- **Minimize the financial risk of company stock holdings.**
- **Know your diversification rights.**
- **Consider optimization of your tax liability upon termination by transferring company stock to taxable nonretirement accounts.**

# CHAPTER 12

## Opportunity Nine—Use 401(k) Loans and Hardship Distribution Features Sparingly

Just as in the classic story "Little Red Riding Hood," some so-called opportunities can disguise themselves as helpful but lead to disastrous consequences. Consider loans and early withdrawals, such as hardship distributions, which can certainly be easy ways to access 401(k) funds before you retire. However, if you aim to meet your financial goals, these "opportunities" are sometimes like the wolf in grandma's clothing. Rather than helping you to achieve your financial goals, loans or early distributions can steer you toward the taxman's jaws. You need to choose wisely when availing yourself of these financial resources.

### PLAN LOANS—ALLY OR ADVERSARY?

Let's examine plan loans. Most 401(k) plans allow participants to borrow money from their accounts, although this is not a legal requirement. You will not have to pay taxes if you take a loan that meets specific duration, amount, and repayment requirements. Loan terms vary, so read the plan information or speak to the administrator.

When you borrow from the plan, you usually sign a loan agreement that includes the loan amount, term, interest rate, fees, and other essential terms. Loans must not exceed the *lesser of $50,000 or 50%* of your *vested* account balance. For example, Erika has a $50,000 vested account balance, which means she can borrow only $25,000 (0.5 × $50,000). However, if her vested account balance was $200,000, she could not take a loan of $100,000 because that exceeds the lesser of $50,000, or 50% of $200,000. The rules vary, but sometimes you can borrow against only your contributions (which are always vested) and not against employer-provided matching or other contributions, such as profit sharing.

Plan loans come with an interest rate set by the plan, often the prime interest rate plus 1%. You generally repay this along with the principal over time with quarterly payments deducted directly from your paycheck and deposited back into your 401(k) account. Most plan loans allow for early repayment without penalties. Most plans also state that five years is the longest period allowed, with the exception of a longer repayment period if you use the money to purchase a primary residence. In that case, you may be able to borrow for twenty-five years.

Before taking out a plan loan, read your SPD thoroughly. It contains essential details about plan loans, like how to start the process, minimum and maximum loan amounts, repayment terms, interest rates, and more. Bear in mind that while plan loans may appear handy, they carry potential drawbacks.

### Missed Market Returns

Once you take out a loan, you will have less money in your account to earn stock market returns. For instance, if Nathan borrows $50,000 from his $200,000 account, he will only have $150,000 left invested. Over the long term, your 401(k) is likely to provide more favorable returns than the interest on the loan you pay to yourself.

The S&P has averaged a return rate of nearly 10% since its inception about one hundred years ago, whereas the prime rate has dipped to nearly 3% and has never reached 9% in the twenty-first century so far as of this writing.[1] Obviously, in a down year for the S&P, the prime rate will be a better option, but no one can predict how the market will do in any year, which is precisely why you need to stay invested over the long term.

If taking out a loan causes you to miss even a single significant market rally, it can have a sizable impact on your retirement accumulations. According to data from Fidelity, if you had invested $10,000 on January 1, 1980, in the S&P 500 index and held it until June 30, 2022, you would have accumulated $1,060,000 (principal plus interest). However, if you missed the five best trading days during this period, your accumulations would have been reduced by 38% to $655,981.[2] Imagine if you'd borrowed money from your retirement account and missed those trading days!

## Accelerated Repayment (and Taxes Due) on Termination

If you leave your job, your 401(k) loan must generally be repaid within ninety days of termination to avoid taxation on your loan amount. Some plans allow terminated employees to continue to repay their loans over the term, but the vast majority do not. Usually, you would have had several years to repay this loan, but your termination now accelerates the repayment, requiring you to come up with significant funds or face steep income taxes on your unpaid loan because the remaining outstanding balance of your loan would be considered a taxable withdrawal from your 401(k). And, if you are under age fifty-nine and a half, you would have that additional 10% penalty tax imposed.

For example, assume you leave your job at age fifty-six with an outstanding loan balance of $30,000 and a retirement account balance of $100,000. If you do not repay the loan in full, you will face significant tax liabilities because the $30,000 outstanding loan becomes due on your termination and is taxable at that point if not repaid. If your tax rate is 25%, you will owe $7,500 ($30,000 × 25%) in income taxes plus an additional $3,000 early withdrawal penalty ($30,000 × 10%). Thus, your tax bill will be $10,500, representing 35% of the $30,000 loan balance because you did not repay the loan when you left your job. Unfortunately, you likely will not have the money to pay the $10,500 in taxes because you had to borrow from the plan in the first place.

## *Limited Allowable Contributions*

Another issue with 401(k) loans is that they may limit how much you can contribute to your plan if you have an outstanding loan, which of course then limits your retirement account's earnings potential. Check your SPD to find out if this applies before you decide to obtain a plan loan.

## *Nondeductible Interest*

The interest you pay on money you borrow from your 401(k) plan, even if used to buy a home, is not deductible on your income tax return, as mortgage interest usually is, because the 401(k) loan is not secured by the home.

## WHEN TO CONSIDER TAKING A 401(k) LOAN

While these drawbacks can discourage taking out a 401(k) loan, there are situations, although relatively rare, when taking out a 401(k) loan is actually an opportunity that makes sense. These loans are easy to obtain, and they often have more attractive interest rates than most other available loans. In fact, according to Bankrate.com, the average personal loan interest rate in October of 2024 was 12.43%, which is higher than the average 401(k) loan rate of prime plus one, which would have been 8% at the same time. Furthermore, the Bankrate article provides that the average personal loan interest rate ranges from 10.73% to 12.5% are those rates granted to borrowers with excellent credit scores.[3] Lower credit scores come with significantly higher rates, with those below 630 (a low credit score) facing average borrowing rates ranging from 28.5% to 32%!

Even with these advantages, 401(k) loans should be used sparingly, but they can be a useful backup in an emergency. The purpose of your savings is to help in difficult situations and not to put you right back into a financial hole. So use the loan in the right situations, but be careful, and don't even consider taking a loan to buy that Porsche you have your eyes on.

**Your retirement plan is for your future and should
be used primarily for this purpose.**

By avoiding loans and early withdrawals as best as you can now,
you can accumulate more assets for the future, affording both peace of
mind and flexibility later in life.

## HARDSHIPS AND OTHER IN-SERVICE DISTRIBUTIONS

Many plans allow you to withdraw some or all of your money while
employed. One common option is the *hardship withdrawal.* IRS rules
allow, but do not require, a hardship withdrawal feature in a 401(k)
plan if an immediate and heavy financial need exists to pay for certain
expenses, including medical, tuition, funeral, or purchase and repair
of a primary residence. You should review your plan's SPD to learn
about all aspects of this feature, if available, including how to apply,
specific hardships permitted, documentation required, and so on.

The withdrawals may help with short-term cash flow issues, but,
like loans, they also have significant downsides. As we've already seen,
you generally cannot take money out of a 401(k) or similar account
before age fifty-nine and a half without owing a 10% tax (some exceptions apply) in addition to ordinary income taxes on the withdrawal.
This can impose a significant tax burden on top of whatever other
hardship you're facing. This incremental tax burden may require you
to withdraw *more* money unless you have other funds to pay the taxes.
For example, if your financial need is $25,000, you would need to with-
draw nearly $38,500 to pay taxes and penalties on that distribution,
assuming a 20% federal income tax rate, 5% for state taxes, and a 10%
penalty.

Some 401(k) plans allow for other (not hardship) withdrawals
while working, which are known as *in-service withdrawals,* including
distributions of matching contributions before age fifty-nine and a
half. I recommend you avoid the temptation and say no, particularly
if you are younger than fifty-nine. Trust me, when you retire, you will
thank me.

Leave your funds in your plan account and let them work for you by compounding over decades. If you run into an unexpected problem, a plan loan is a better option than a hardship withdrawal, particularly if you are younger than fifty-nine and a half. But it is always wise to look for alternatives before removing assets from your 401(k) plan by borrowing or withdrawing.

Alternatives you may want to consider to help bridge tough financial times include the following:

*Establishing an emergency fund:* You set aside money in a savings account to cover unexpected expenses or financial emergencies, such as a job loss or medical expenses. This fund acts as a financial safety net and can help you avoid the need to borrow or withdraw from your retirement savings. Most experts recommend maintaining three to twelve months' worth of living expenses in a cash account to cover financial emergencies or unplanned expenses without liquidating your investments or borrowing money.[4]

*Reducing your expenses:* By cutting back on nonessential expenses, you might be able to free up some money to handle financial challenges.

*Exploring low-interest loans:* While taking on debt is not ideal, it might be a better option in some cases than taking a loan from your 401(k). For example, home equity loans might offer favorable interest rates and will not impact your retirement savings. You also are able to deduct the interest on equity loans.

## SUMMARY

- **Although 401(k) loans are easy to obtain and sometimes have lower interest rates, they have several drawbacks and should generally be avoided:**
  - » **They reduce your retirement funds available for investment.**
  - » **They can lead to accelerated repayment and significant tax liabilities upon termination of employment.**

>> **They may restrict the amount you can con-
   tribute to your 401(k) while the loan is
   outstanding.**
>> **Interest on 401(k) loans is not deductible for
   tax purposes.**

- **Hardship and other early withdrawals should also be
  avoided except as a last resort.**

# CHAPTER 13

## Opportunity Ten—Secure Your Legacy and the Future for Your Loved Ones

Life is unpredictable, and we never know what the future may bring. When thinking about retirement planning, some people want their money to last and provide flexibility for the next generation, but they live longer than anticipated. Others may, unfortunately, pass away earlier than expected and don't have their affairs in order.

It's never pleasant to think about these things, and younger adults rarely give this a thought, but the old saying "Nothing is certain except death and taxes" is relevant here—for everyone. With that in mind, this chapter focuses on safeguarding the interests of your loved ones—your beneficiaries—after your death. Whether your goal is to secure your spouse's future or create a nest egg for your children, we'll provide you with the know-how to achieve that. Plus, we'll help you dodge common obstacles and navigate confusing rules, ensuring your assets transfer according to your wishes. This way, you can avoid the situation where unintended people inherit your assets, giving you peace of mind about your family's future and your legacy.

## THE BENEFICIARY DESIGNATION FORM

The first step toward ensuring their future is for you to complete a *beneficiary designation*. This document is a tool used within 401(k) plans and IRAs (which are addressed in detail in chapter 14) to identify your successors. While it may appear straightforward, it does require regular, careful attention to set things up correctly and to make modifications when necessary, especially during life changes such as death, birth, marriage, divorce, or separation. Many people make the mistake of assuming that their will determines who will inherit their assets on death. However, *your will does not apply to certain accounts and policies*—including 401(k)s, IRAs, life insurance policies, and certain bank and brokerage accounts (generally titled transfer-on-death accounts). The succession of assets in these accounts and policies is controlled by beneficiary designations, rather than wills, to determine who will inherit your account or policy.

And this form must be completed correctly to ensure your intentions are carried out. If there are mistakes, your assets could end up with an ex-spouse, or they could get caught up in a court battle. This is a growing problem as more Americans maintain several accounts and have greater asset holdings in retirement accounts.[1] To make this even more confusing, the rules that apply to beneficiary designations are different for 401(k) plans and IRAs.

If you have a 401(k) plan without a completed beneficiary designation, your spouse (if you're married) will automatically become your beneficiary. If you wish to designate someone else, your spouse *must consent* on the form in the presence of a notary. If you aren't married, you can use the beneficiary designation form to name your beneficiaries. If you don't, your account will follow the plan's rules, commonly directing assets in this order: spouse, children, parents, and estate. Updating this form can save your beneficiaries from a potentially lengthy, expensive court process. It can also help them defer taxes because, without a designated beneficiary, the entire amount must be paid to the beneficiary within five years of the owner's death, with *taxes due at distribution*. But if there is a designated beneficiary, the five-year rule can be extended, lengthening the deferral of taxes.

IRAs, on the other hand, allow you to name someone other than your spouse as a beneficiary without spousal consent in most states, except if you reside in a *community-property state*, such as Texas or California.[2] If no beneficiary is listed or designated, the provisions of the IRA agreement determine who inherits an IRA.[3] For example, some agreements provide that, in the absence of a designated beneficiary, the surviving spouse is the beneficiary, and if there is no surviving spouse, the estate is the beneficiary. Under that scenario, the account's distribution is governed by a will or, if there is no will, by state law.

> **Designating beneficiaries for your 401(k) and IRA ensures your assets go to the people you choose through a relatively smooth and timely process.**

By avoiding state laws or default arrangements set forth by the plans, which might not align with your wishes, and by allowing assets to bypass courts, you can save time, cost, and unnecessary stress for your loved ones. Naming beneficiaries also helps prevent disputes and clarifies your intentions, ensuring a smooth transfer of assets. And the designation is also a best practice because it provides financial security and can offer tax advantages to those who inherit your retirement accounts.

The most common mistakes with beneficiary designations include not naming a primary or contingent beneficiary, failing to review and update the designations after life events (death, birth, marriage, divorce, or separation), and not following the instructions on the designation.

## PRIMARY AND CONTINGENT BENEFICIARIES

When enrolling in a 401(k) plan, you can name a primary and a contingent beneficiary. *The primary beneficiary* is the first to receive your benefits when you pass away, while the *contingent beneficiaries* will inherit only if the primary beneficiary predeceases you. Failing to name a primary and contingent beneficiary is one of the most common mistakes made with beneficiary designations.

Another crucial consideration to watch out for is the often-overlooked clause in *some* 401(k) and IRA forms or instructions stating that contingent beneficiaries will receive a distribution only if *all* primary beneficiaries have passed away before the account owner. This can lead to unintentional transfers of assets unless you are careful. Take the case of Ann, a single mother with two children, Claire and Dave, and two grandchildren, Carl (Claire's son) and Dexter (Dave's son). Ann is the 401(k) account owner and her primary beneficiaries are Claire and Dave, while her contingent beneficiaries are her grandchildren Carl (if Claire predeceases Ann) and Dexter (if Dave predeceases Ann). As it turned out, Dave died a year before Ann, and her entire account passed to her surviving daughter, Claire, instead of being split between Claire and Dexter. This was because, despite her intention, the beneficiary designation form states that contingent beneficiaries do not inherit unless there are *no* primary beneficiaries alive at the time of the 401(k) owner's death. Ann could have prevented this result by changing her beneficiary designation after Dave's death to name Dexter as one of two primary beneficiaries so that half of the account would go to him and the other half to Claire as the other primary beneficiary.

## UPDATE AFTER MAJOR LIFE EVENTS

Eric and Georgette's story shows the importance of reviewing your beneficiary designations after divorce. Eric and Georgette were briefly married. During the marriage, she named Eric as the beneficiary of her 401(k) account. After the divorce, Georgette forgot to update her designated beneficiary form. Years later, Georgette passed away and had never remarried. Eric, therefore, inherited her 401(k) balance because he was the named beneficiary on her form. Georgette could have prevented her ex-spouse from receiving her 401(k) account by updating her beneficiary designation form before her death.

Another common problem occurs after a divorce when someone changes his beneficiary designation to name his children and remarries a few years later. For example, Larry gets divorced and then names his daughter, Chloe, as his beneficiary. Larry marries Kim several years later. He wants to leave his 401(k) account to Chloe, not Kim. Larry never updated his form naming Chloe because she is his intended beneficiary. Unfortunately, when Larry dies, Kim will inherit his account because, as we discussed above, Kim, Larry's spouse, is automatically the beneficiary unless she signs an updated consent form in the presence of a notary.

Divorce is one of the most common life events that should trigger a review of your designated beneficiary form. Other events include death of a beneficiary, birth of a child, marriage, or separation. It is crucial to stay vigilant, especially considering your 401(k) account is likely one of your most valuable assets, and a mistake could incur a hefty cost for you and your loved ones.

Next, we will cover a possible way to make the beneficiary process easier. Using a *per stirpes* designation, problems related to unintended wealth transfers or accidental disinheritance, particularly when families undergo transitions like death or divorce, can be mitigated.


## PER STIRPES DISTRIBUTIONS

Let's look at another example of a problem caused by failing to properly update a beneficiary designation form after a major life event. Meet Mario, who was married with two kids. Mario's wife, Janet, was his primary beneficiary, designated to receive 100% of his account upon his death. His children, Selina and Marta, were named his contingent beneficiaries to split his account equally should Janet pass before him.

What actually happened was that both Janet and Selina predeceased Mario. That meant his surviving daughter, Marta, would receive 100% of Mario's account when he passed because she is the only remaining beneficiary. But Selina had one child, Sam, and Mario wanted to leave Selina's half to Sam. He even expressed this in writing in his will. Unfortunately, Mario never changed his beneficiary designation form after Janet and Selina died. Because the beneficiary designation form controls his 401(k) assets and not Mario's will, the result was an unintended gift to Marta at the expense of Selina's child.

Many people intend to divide their account on death, like Mario, so that if a beneficiary predeceases the account owner, the beneficiary's share of the assets is distributed equally among their children (the children step into their parents' shoes). A per stirpes designation accomplishes this. For instance, Mario's beneficiary form could have stated the following:

*My primary beneficiary is my wife if she survives me; if not, my contingent beneficiaries are my descendants (children, grandchildren, etc.) who survive me, per stirpes.*

In this case, Marta receives her half, and Sam steps into Selina's shoes and receives her half. The per stirpes approach helps to prevent the issues described above, where Selina dies without a per stirpes designation.

Mario could have accomplished the same thing if he had remembered to complete an updated beneficiary form naming Selina's children *and* Marta as beneficiaries when Janet and Selina died as equal primary beneficiaries. The per stirpes approach is less prone to error because no changes are needed after certain life events, minimizing unintended transfers.

In another example, Mark, an engineer at General Motors, completed a per stirpes beneficiary designation for his 401(k) account. He wanted to leave his $300,000 account to his children, Naomi and Roger, per stirpes. Although Naomi predeceased him, the designation ensured that Mark's account was split evenly between his son, Roger, and Naomi's son, Nate. If Mark had not used the per stirpes designation and had forgotten to update the designation form after Naomi's death, Roger would have inherited Mark's full $300,000 account, and Nate would not have received any of the retirement inheritance.

Per stirpes designations can be made when you enroll in your plan in some but not all plans. If a per stirpes designation interests you, find out from your plan administrator if you can make this designation under your plan. It is a simple way to leave your assets to your loved ones and is far less prone to error. I use a per stirpes designation in my personal estate planning because, in my view, it seems fair.

Some 401(k) plans and IRAs do not permit per stirpes designations. However, with diligence in updating your beneficiary designations following a change in your family's status, you can still ensure your assets are distributed according to your wishes.

The lesson: Read, understand, and fill out the beneficiary designation form, paying close attention to instructions. Do not hesitate to seek clarification from your plan or IRA administrator, as these matters can be tricky, and mistakes are easy to make. Also, keep your beneficiary designation forms organized with your other vital documents, such as life insurance policies, wills, and others, in a file that you or your loved ones can easily find. (See appendix E for information on critical documents and insurance coverages.)

## SUMMARY

- **Ensure your intentions are honored by carefully completing your beneficiary designation form, which governs how your retirement assets will be distributed upon death.**
- **Carefully name your primary and contingent beneficiaries.**
- **Review and update your form after any major life event (marriage, birth, death, divorce, or separation).**
- **Consider using a per stirpes designation to ensure that your intentions are followed in the event one of your beneficiaries predeceases you.**

# CHAPTER 14

## Opportunity Eleven—No 401(k)?
## No Problem—Open an IRA!

My Uncle Dave had a knack for sharing wisdom, especially regarding investing. One piece of advice he gave me as a kid stuck with me: "Start an IRA as soon as you earn your first dollar." I took his advice to heart and opened an *individual retirement account (IRA)*. The results were fantastic. The simple act of saving early and watching how compounding works helped solidify my financial future. In addition, I learned the power of leveraging tax-advantaged investing because IRA contributions are *tax deductible*, and the earnings in those accounts are not taxed until decades later when I would need them for retirement. An IRA can help solidify yours as well!

According to the US Bureau of Labor Statistics, in 2024, 72% of private industry provided employees access to a defined contribution plan or defined benefit plan.[1] If you are not eligible for an employer-sponsored plan, such as a 401(k) or other defined contribution plan, you are eligible to participate in an IRA. Introduced in 1974 through ERISA, traditional IRAs were designed to boost savings by allowing them to grow tax-free until withdrawn. They are handy today, particularly if you cannot access a 401(k) plan or are self-employed. Maybe it is time you get in on the action!

Although IRAs are widely available, only 14% of family units contribute to IRAs, so there is room for more folks to take advantage of this fantastic saving opportunity.[2] Interestingly, much of the money currently sitting in IRAs came from being rolled over from 401(k) plans, not from individual contributions to an IRA. It's a bit surprising that more people aren't involved because establishing an IRA is simple. Vanguard, Fidelity, and Schwab offer low-cost index investing and have good customer service, based on my experience, but other brokerage firms also offer IRA accounts. Because IRAs can be an important tool for ensuring your financial security in retirement, this chapter is dedicated to understanding them. We will cover when to use an IRA, how it differs from a 401(k), common mistakes to avoid, and the different types of IRAs, such as traditional IRAs and Roth IRAs. Without further delay, let us jump into the world of IRAs.

## TRADITIONAL IRA

This type of retirement account is similar to the traditional 401(k); contributions are tax deductible in both these arrangements, money grows tax-free until withdrawn, and withdrawals before age fifty-nine and a half may result in a 10% early withdrawal penalty. Although IRAs have lower contribution limits and no employer matching, they offer advantages, including offering many more investment options and the ability to make contributions for a particular year after the year-end, up until the federal tax filing deadline of April 15 of the following year. This is especially helpful for folks who want to deposit their year-end bonus into their IRAs.

One key consideration when deciding whether to contribute to an IRA is that income limits may apply to the *deductibility* of your contribution. In 2024, you could contribute to your traditional IRA up to $7,000 if you were under fifty and up to $8,000 if you were age fifty or older, *without regard to your income* as long as you were *not* eligible for an employer-sponsored retirement plan.

However, if you or your spouse is *eligible* for an employer's plan, such as a 401(k), whether or not you contribute to the 401(k) plan, your income will determine how much you can contribute to your traditional IRA. For example, Alex is eligible for his company 401(k) plan but decides not to participate. If he chooses to fund a traditional IRA, he will be subject to income limits because he is eligible to participate in the company plan, regardless of his participation decision.

If you or your spouse was eligible for an employer plan, married, and filed taxes together in 2024, a fully deductible contribution of $7,000 (or $8,000, depending on your age) was allowed if your *modified adjusted gross income (MAGI)* was $123,000 or less. Your deduction was phased out if your MAGI exceeded $123,000 and was eliminated at $143,000. If you were single, the deduction was phased out when your MAGI exceeded $77,000 and was eliminated at $87,000. The 2024 contribution limits of $7,000 or $8,000 and the MAGI limits are adjusted annually. Please check the limits each year. The IRS announces the limits for each year on its website, IRS.gov, about two months before the beginning of each year. You can google IRA limits for any year and find the IRS announcement on this website before the start of any year.

Many taxpayers are not familiar with the concept of MAGI. It is based on your adjusted gross income (AGI), as reported on your individual income tax return (Form 1040), and then modified by adding back certain deductions (or subtracting certain income items). For many people, MAGI may simply equal their AGI plus any student loan interest that you had deducted when calculating your taxes. Other adjustments to AGI include savings bond interest, foreign-earned income, housing exclusion and deductions, employer-provided adoption benefits, Social Security benefits excluded from taxable income, and passive losses. IRS Publication 590 can guide you through the calculation. However, due to its complexity, you may want to consult with your accountant for assistance.

Another restriction with traditional IRA contributions is that they may be made only by people who report *earned income* for tax purposes, which includes wages, salaries, tips, and other forms of work income. Investment income, such as dividends from stock investments, interest from savings accounts, or other sources of *unearned income*, do not qualify as a basis for a contribution.

For example, Karen had a job as a marketing coordinator and earned $50,000 in salary last year. She contributed $6,000 of her earned income to her IRA, which is allowed because her salary is considered earned income. On the other hand, Alain received $2,000 last year from dividends and interest. However, since Alain didn't have a job and earned no wages or salary, this income is considered investment income, not earned income, so he cannot contribute to an IRA.

## ROTH IRA

Roth IRAs are similar to traditional IRAs, except that Roth contributions are *not* tax deductible, and income limits apply to your contribution, whether or not you or your spouse is eligible for an employer's plan. If you were married and filed taxes together in 2024, a Roth contribution of $7,000 if you were under age fifty (and up to $8,000 if you were fifty or over) was permitted. Your deduction would phase out if your MAGI exceeded $230,000 and is eliminated at $240,000. If you were single, the $7,000 (or $8,000) phases out when your MAGI exceeded $146,000 and disappeared at $161,000.

If you are eligible for a Roth IRA and a traditional IRA and want to decide which is best for you, my recommendation is as follows: If the tax rate at the time of contribution is less than that at retirement, opt for a Roth and pay less tax on the contribution. If the tax rate at the time of distribution is projected to be less than at the time of contribution, opt for traditional and pay less tax at distribution. There is no impact if the tax rate is the same at the time of contribution and distribution. See chapter 6 for an in-depth discussion of the Roth versus traditional contribution decision as it applies to 401(k) contributions. Although the IRA has a smaller contribution limit than the 401(k) plan does, the concepts and recommendations apply.

## NONDEDUCTIBLE IRA

Individuals who cannot deduct traditional IRA contributions due to the limits described in table 5 may make nondeductible contributions.[3]

While these IRAs don't provide an immediate tax deduction for the contribution, they offer tax-deferred growth, meaning earnings are not taxed until you take a distribution. The contribution limits are the same as for other IRAs: $7,000 or $8,000 in 2024, depending on your age. And, like other types of IRAs, contributions must come from earned income. Nondeductible IRAs can be converted to a Roth IRA, allowing for tax-free withdrawals and growth, provided certain requirements are met. However, in most cases, it is more beneficial to contribute to a Roth IRA rather than make nondeductible contributions to a traditional IRA. A Roth IRA's eligibility is subject to higher income thresholds than traditional IRA deduction requirements (see tables 5 and 6). If you can't make Roth IRAs due to the limits described in table 6, see the backdoor IRA discussion below.

If you are a high-income employee, the nondeductible IRA has some important disadvantages in addition to the loss of an immediate tax deduction:

*Complex recordkeeping:* Careful tracking of contributions is required using Form 8606, which must be filed each year contributions are made or distributions are received.

*Complex distribution rules:* Distributions include both taxable and nontaxable portions, determined by the ratio of your account's earnings to the account balance, which makes tax reporting tricky. For instance, if Gail contributed $40,000 to her nondeductible IRA and the account grew to $60,000, a $10,000 distribution would include both taxable and nontaxable amounts based on the earnings-to-principal ratio. In this case, it would be assumed that one-third of her account balance stemmed from earnings and two-thirds originated from her contributions (income already taxed). Therefore, 33% of the distribution, or approximately $3,333, would be considered taxable.

*Penalty taxes:* Withdrawals before age fifty-nine and a half may be subject to a 10% penalty on the earnings portion of the distribution.

Overall, while nondeductible IRAs offer tax-deferred growth and the option to convert to a Roth IRA, they come with complexities that may not make them suitable for everyone. Careful consideration of your financial situation and retirement goals is necessary to determine whether this option is right for you. I believe they are often not worth the effort; I like things simpler than this. It's great to save, but don't drive yourself crazy with complicated options.

## ROTH CONVERSIONS

Everyone who has funds in a traditional or nondeductible IRA, regardless of income, can convert to a Roth IRA. This might make sense if you expect your tax rates to rise because it would be better to pay taxes on the money converted now at lower rates, as taxable income, than later when you withdraw it after retirement at higher rates.

However, because the amount converted is considered taxable income, this transaction could move you into a higher tax bracket, so you need to be careful. Younger people, or those who expect lower taxable income at conversion than they expect in the future, will benefit most from this action.

One strategy for a Roth conversion is to convert only enough from your traditional IRA to stay within your current tax bracket and avoid flowing into the next bracket. For example, assume you are single and have a taxable income of $90,000. You also have $50,000 in a traditional IRA that you would like to convert to a Roth. Your taxable income placed you in a 22% marginal tax bracket in 2024, and the next bracket, with a tax rate of 24%, began at an income level of $101,526. You could have initiated a conversion of up to $11,525 for that year, bringing your balance up to that level, and remain in the 22% bracket. You would then continue converting the remaining balance in subsequent years, subject to your income level and current tax rates. Roth IRA conversions make the most sense if you expect to be in a higher tax bracket after you retire.

## BACKDOOR ROTH IRA

A backdoor Roth IRA is a method for high earners to fund a Roth IRA by making nondeductible contributions to a traditional IRA and converting the funds to a Roth IRA. High earners are prohibited from making direct Roth IRA contributions if their income exceeds certain limits (see table 6). Roth accounts offer tax-free growth, tax-free withdrawals in retirement, and no required minimum distributions (RMDs).

Taxes on a backdoor Roth IRA conversion can be confusing,

especially if you have several traditional IRAs with both deductible and nondeductible contributions. Generally, earnings are taxable at conversion, while nondeductible contributions are not. However, the IRS uses a rule that treats all your traditional IRAs as a single IRA when calculating taxes, so you can't select only nondeductible contributions to convert.

For instance, if your IRAs total $100,000 and 80% of the balance consists of taxable contributions and earnings, converting $10,000 of after-tax contribution would mean $8,000 is considered taxable. There is a workaround by rolling over the $80,000 taxable contributions and earnings to your employer's 401(k) plan before the conversion, if permitted. In addition, you need to file IRS Form 8606 to track nondeductible contributions.

A backdoor Roth IRA has important trade-offs. Pros include tax-free withdrawals in retirement and no RMDs during your lifetime. Cons include potential taxes on converted earnings and deductible contributions, the risk of being pushed into a higher tax bracket, and the five-year rule, which imposes restrictions and possible penalties on early withdrawals of converted amounts.

Because of the complexity involved, I suggest consulting with a tax professional for advice on whether this makes sense and to make sure the rules are followed. As explained above, I am not a fan of this strategy due to its complexities.

## COMPARING 401(k)S AND IRAS

By now you may be finding it hard to discern among traditional 401(k)s, traditional IRAs, Roth 401(k)s, and Roth IRAs. These plans share several features but also have key differences. Table 4 offers an easy way to review the basics.

## Table 4. Comparison of 401(k) and IRA plans

| | Traditional 401(k) | Roth 401(k) | Traditional IRA | Roth IRA |
|---|---|---|---|---|
| Number of investment options | Limited, as offered by the plan | Limited, as offered by the plan | Many, as long as not prohibited | Many, as long as not prohibited |
| Participation | Employees subject to eligibility rules | Employees subject to eligibility rules | Anyone with earned income; income limits apply if eligible for 401(k) or other plan | Anyone with earned income; income limits apply |
| Tax effect of contribution | Tax deductible | Taxable as ordinary income | Tax deductible | Taxable as ordinary income |
| Contribution limits (2024) | $23,000 ($30,500 age 50 or over) | $23,000 ($30,500 age 50 or over) | $7,000 ($8,000 age 50 or over) if not eligible for 401(k); if eligible, contribution limits subject to MAGI | $7,000 ($8,000 age 50 or over) subject to MAGI |
| RMDs | Yes | After owner's death | Yes | After owner's death |
| Distributions | Taxable as ordinary income | Tax-free | Taxable as ordinary income | Tax-free |
| Loans | Yes, if plan allows | Yes, if plan allows | No | No |
| Beneficiaries | Anyone, with spouse's consent | Anyone, with spouse's consent | Anyone, subject to state law | Anyone, subject to state law |

## KEY STRATEGIES FOR TRADITIONAL AND ROTH IRAS

Let's bring it all together:

**IRAs can benefit nearly everyone, whether supplementing their 401(k) savings or focusing solely on individual accounts to help ensure a more flexible and secure financial future.**

As you prepare to set up or continue to invest in your IRA, you might want to explore several IRA-related strategies.

*Flying solo:* If you are single and don't meet eligibility requirements for your employer plan, or your employer does not offer a plan, you can contribute the full amount to a traditional IRA each year without regard to your income because that restriction only applies if a 401(k) is available to you. You may also qualify for a Roth IRA, depending on your earnings (MAGI). But you do need to be careful and not *overcontribute.* In 2024, the maximum contribution limit for *all* of your IRAs is the *lesser of* $7,000 ($8,000 if you are fifty or older) or your *taxable income from a job* (earned income as opposed to unearned income, such as from interest or other investments) for the year. For example, Paul, an employee of Apple, can contribute $3,500 to a traditional IRA and $3,500 to a Roth IRA if eligible for both types of IRAs and if he has earned income at least equal to $7,000. He can also contribute $7,000 to a single Roth *or* a traditional IRA, but he cannot exceed the limit of $7,000 on an aggregate basis if he contributes to more than one IRA during the year.

*Double the fun:* If you are married and neither you nor your spouse are eligible for an employer plan, you can each max out contributions to a tax-deductible traditional IRA. If either of you are eligible for an employer plan, you can still make a contribution up to the $7,000 or $8,000 limit to a Roth (i.e., nondeductible) plan, depending on your combined income (MAGI). Table 5 provides these limits. Each spouse should be careful not to exceed the limits of the *lesser of* $7,000 (or $8,000) or their *taxable income* for the year across all their IRAs.

*Nonworking spouse? No problem!* The IRS permits exceptions for nonworking spouses. Suppose your earnings are sufficient to cover contributions for yourself and your spouse, you file a joint tax return, neither of you are eligible to participate in any employer-sponsored retirement plan, and your spouse has no earned income but is otherwise eligible to participate in an IRA. If you were both under fifty, you could have saved up to $14,000 for 2024 on a combined basis—or $16,000 if you were both fifty or older!

For example, assume Bill is fifty years old and earned $70,000 in taxable (earned) income. Bill's wife, Cheryl, is also over fifty, does not work, and has no earned income. Since Bill meets the "fifty or over" rule and is not eligible to participate in any retirement plan, he can contribute up to $8,000 to a traditional IRA, and Cheryl can also contribute $8,000, even though she has no earned income since Bill's earned income of $70,000 is enough to cover both contributions as it is greater than the $16,000 maximum allowed for the two of them taken together. They can each contribute to a Roth or a traditional IRA and even split their contributions between the two types, so long as the total does not exceed $8,000 for either of them.

*Power couple with employer plans:* If you and your spouse are eligible to participate in an employer-sponsored retirement plan, aim to maximize those contributions. This is an excellent move if you can afford it. Depending on your MAGI, you can also contribute to a Roth IRA in addition to the 401(k) contributions. In this case, Harvey can contribute $23,000 ($30,500 with a catch-up) to his employer's 401(k), and Nancy can contribute the same amount to her employer's plan, for a combined $61,000 since they are both over fifty. Depending on their income levels and what they can afford, they may each be able to contribute an additional $8,000 to a Roth IRA.

*A sweet child:* A Roth IRA makes sense for those who are young. Once a child or young adult has earned income, they can contribute to an IRA as long as their taxable income is equal to or greater than the contribution. If a Roth IRA is used, the child can get many decades of compounded tax-free income at no tax cost for life because they generally pay little or no income tax. According to a recent article in *The Wall Street Journal*, Roth IRAs for teenagers are becoming more common.[4]

Some parents set up custodial Roth accounts for their children at a financial institution, like a brokerage firm, which they manage for the benefit of their minor children (under the age of eighteen to twenty-one as determined by state law). Fidelity reports that these Roth IRAs experienced a 28% growth in June 2023 compared to the previous year, and the typical age for children with these types of accounts is 13.7 years.[5] When the child is no longer a minor, the IRA is legally theirs and not controlled by the parent. Hopefully, they won't cash out and go on a spree.

*Splitting between Roth and traditional IRAs:* You can divide your contributions, if eligible, for both Roth and traditional IRAs. However, remember, your combined contributions across all IRAs are limited; in 2024, the maximum was $7,000 (or $8,000 if fifty or older). You also cannot contribute more to your Roth or traditional IRA annually than your yearly earned income.

## COMMON IRA MISTAKES

While IRA plans can be a beneficial part of your retirement savings strategy, they can also cause pain. Watch out for these problems so your savings won't wane.

*Overcontributions:* The IRS will impose a 6% tax penalty if you contribute too much to your IRA. Although there are several ways to correct excess contributions and to avoid the excess tax entirely in future years, it's best to monitor your contributions along the way.

*Not taking required minimum distributions (RMDs):* Traditional retirement accounts, including traditional IRAs, require that you take out distributions when you reach a certain age. Failure to do so can cause significant penalty taxes, generally at age seventy-three, or beginning in 2033, at age seventy-five (although this is not applicable to Roth contributions and earnings). If you are careless, inheriting an IRA (Roth or traditional) can cause unnecessary tax burdens for others if you don't take RMDs as required (generally within ten years of the owner's death). Chapter 17 covers this subject in detail.

## TABLES OF IRA DEDUCTION AND CONTRIBUTION LIMITS

The deduction and contribution limits can be confusing. Tables 5 and 6 summarize this information for traditional and Roth IRAs for 2024. Data for later years can be found on many different websites.

*Traditional IRA:* Income limits do not apply if you are *not* eligible to participate in a 401(k) plan or other employer plan, and you can contribute the maximum of $7,000 or $8,000 in 2024. If income limits apply and your MAGI for a particular filing status is below $77,000 (if single or head of household, for example), you can fully contribute for the year. If your MAGI rises, you may still contribute to your IRA, but the *deductibility* of your contributions may decrease.

Again, in the case of a *traditional IRA*, these income requirements *only apply if you are eligible to participate in a 401(k) plan* or another employer plan. If not, no income limits apply, although the contribution deductions are still limited to a maximum of $7,000 or $8,000.

*Roth IRA:* Contributions are limited based on income and filing status *regardless* of whether you are eligible to participate in a 401(k) or another employer plan.

*Table 5. Traditional IRA deduction limits (2024)[6]*

| Filing status | Modified adjusted gross income | Deduction limit |
|---|---|---|
| Single or head of household | $77,000 or less | Full deduction |
| Single or head of household | Greater than $77,000 but less than $87,000 | Only a portion of your contribution |
| Single or head of household | $87,000 or more | No deduction |
| Married filing jointly or qualifying widow(er) | $123,000 or less | Full deduction |
| Married filing jointly or qualifying widow(er) | More than $123,000 but less than $143,000 | Only a portion of your contribution |
| Married filing jointly or qualifying widow(er) | $143,000 or more | No deduction |
| Married filing separately | Less than $10,000 | Only a portion of your contribution |
| Married filing separately | $10,000 or more | No deduction |

*Table 6. Roth IRA contribution limits (2024)*[7]

| Filing status | Modified adjusted gross income | Contribution limit |
|---|---|---|
| Single, head of household, or married filing separately and lived with spouse at any time during the year | Less than $146,000 | $7,000 or $8,000 |
| Single, head of household, or married filing separately and lived with spouse at any time during the year | More than $146,000 but less than $161,000 | Reduced amount |
| Single, head of household, or married filing separately and lived with spouse at any time during the year | $161,000 or more | No contribution allowed |
| Married filing jointly or qualifying widow(er) | Less than $230,000 | $7,000 or $8,000 |
| Married filing jointly or qualifying widow(er) | More than $230,000 but less than $240,000 | Reduced amount |
| Married filing jointly or qualifying widow(er) | $240,000 or more | No contribution allowed |
| Married filing separately | Less than $10,000 | Reduced amount |
| Married filing separately | $10,000 or more | No contribution allowed |

## IRAS FOR SELF-EMPLOYED INDIVIDUALS AND SMALL BUSINESS OWNERS

Entrepreneurs, sole practitioners, and people working in the fast-growing gig economy need options for retirement planning too. By some estimates, the gig economy, with its flexible or temporary jobs, will account for over 50% of the workforce in 2028. Many of these workers do not have access to 401(k) plans through an employer.

If you work for yourself, you can consider setting up your own retirement plan. So far, this chapter has provided a high-level overview of several options available to you. For the self-employed and small business owner, in this current section I hope to motivate you to explore your options. Through careful planning and implementing the right approach, you will be on your way to more flexibility and a secure retirement.

*The IRA:* As discussed above, an IRA is as easy as it gets and can be used by small business owners who have no employees. Contributions are limited to $7,000 in 2024 ($8,000 for age fifty or older).

*Payroll deduction IRA:* Employees set up their own traditional or Roth IRAs and authorize employers to deduct contributions from their paychecks. This option may create goodwill with employees, with little cost or administrative responsibilities for the business owner.

*Simplified employee pension (SEP) plan:* Employer contributions are made equally for all employees and are limited to the lesser of 25% of compensation or $69,000 (in 2024). Easy to set up and flexible, these plans operate with low administrative costs. No traditional or Roth contributions can be made, but these plans have the same tax treatment as an IRA account. These plans often appeal to small companies with no or few employees.

*Simple IRA:* Best for companies with fewer than one hundred employees, this plan requires either employer-matching contributions at 3% of compensation or 2% nonmatching contributions. Employees are 100% vested, and in 2024, employee contributions were limited to $16,000 with a $3,500 catch-up opportunity. These plans have the same tax treatment as traditional IRAs and are easy to set up and run. Contributions are required and can be expensive.

*Solo 401(k):* Difficult and expensive to set up and maintain, but this plan, which offers high contribution limits, may be appropriate for the self-employed person with no employees, except if the spouse is the sole employee. Ideal if the business owner is very successful, as the contributions, which are made as both employer and employee portions, have high limits ($23,000 with a $7,500 catch-up opportunity in 2024). Self-employed individuals can contribute up to 25% of net earnings—essentially your profit minus half of your self-employment taxes.

# SUMMARY

- IRAs can be an important component of a well-rounded retirement savings strategy.
- Consider a traditional IRA, especially if you are not eligible for an employer's plan.
- Consider a Roth IRA for retirement or a Roth conversion, depending on taxable income and tax rates.
- Explore key IRA strategies, depending on your age, marital status, and income levels, for flexibility and security in your financial future.
- Avoid common, costly IRA mistakes, such as over-contributing or not taking out required minimum distributions.
- Set up your own IRA if you are working on your own or if you own a small business.

# PART III

Problems

# CHAPTER 15

## Problem One—Illegally Left Out?

Imagine the excitement of starting a new part-time job only to be told that you can't join the company's retirement plan. It's a disappointment, to say the least, but don't let it discourage you. There might be a way for you to join the party.

This problem reminds me of my yearly attempt to get tickets for the US Open Tennis Championships in New York City. Every year, tickets go on sale early. The sale starts at 9 a.m. sharp on a preannounced date. My wife and I carefully prepare, starting at 8:30 a.m., making sure our computers are ready. We test the internet connection, check our passwords, and double-check the sale date. Attending the US Open has become an annual tradition for us. We love walking around the grounds and watching our favorite players together with up-and-coming talent.

Unfortunately, we sometimes cannot get tickets despite our efforts because they sell out within minutes directly from the US Open. When that happens, we consider the ridiculous prices on the secondary market, where tickets are resold at a significant markup from the already high-priced direct market variety. This system feels unfair and excludes many people who want to attend and follow the rules. I often suspect some people know how to game the system, although I have no proof.

You might ask, "What does this have to do with my 401(k)?" The bridge is the unfairness of being excluded. Just as fans are denied tickets, some employees are unfairly excluded from participating in 401(k), profit-sharing, and other plans, even though the IRS has flagged this issue as sometimes impermissible. Unlike the ticket situation, where you can theoretically buy your way in, these employees face a more serious problem because their exclusion from the retirement plans means the plan isn't operating according to its legally required terms. And the employees are losing the opportunity to set aside and grow funds for retirement. Let's look at where this issue often arises and explore possible solutions.

## PART-TIME WORKERS BEWARE

Part-time employees, including hourly workers, salaried part-time workers, interns, students, on-call employees, and contingent workers, often face improper exclusion from retirement plans. In fact, according to the IRS, *improperly* excluding these workers is one of the most common mistakes companies make. Error number 6 on the IRS 401(k) Fix-It Guide, which is supposed to help plans follow the law, deals with improperly not providing eligible employees the opportunity to make employee contributions.[1] The IRS states in this guide, "Your 401(k) plan document should contain a definition of 'employee' and provide requirements for when employees must become plan participants eligible to make elective deferrals. Employers sometimes assume the plan does not cover certain employees, such as part-time employees."[2] If you find yourself excluded from your plan, you may be able to correct it, particularly if you are not employed full-time.

For example, a company's 401(k) plan sometimes states that all employees are covered, but the plan administrator excludes part-time employees from participating despite the plan language. Here, the plan administrator takes action that directly conflicts with the plan terms. If this is discovered, the administrative practice needs to be corrected, and the affected employees may even be entitled to employer contributions to correct past errors. If you're a part-time employee denied retirement plan participation, it's time to investigate! Just as you review your bank accounts and bills for accuracy, it is worth investing a bit of time to determine whether your exclusion is consistent with the written plan terms.

Because part-time employee participation and exclusion issues are common, I always start by interviewing the staff members responsible for the plan when reviewing this issue for a company. This is how the conversation sometimes unfolds:

*Me: Are all employees eligible to participate in the plan?*

*Staff member: Yes.*

*Me: Are part-time employees eligible to participate?*

*Staff member: No.*

Obviously, I think *something is wrong here*. On the one hand, they say all employees are eligible, but then they say part-time employees are not. Which is it?

Plan administrators can make mistakes even when applying basic plan provisions. If your plan administrator informs you that you are not eligible, don't immediately assume this is the case. The written terms are not always followed, and mistakes can happen—sometimes going back many years before they are caught and corrected. Lina was one such employee who was improperly denied participation in her company's plan for *three* years until the mistake was uncovered and corrected. Fortunately, corrective benefit payments were made to correct the mistake, and she could participate going forward.

So how do you ensure your eligibility? Your first step is to send a letter requesting a copy of your plan document and SPD from your plan administrator. The SPD may be accessible online. Understanding these documents is key to ensuring your rights and benefits.

Another common issue occurs when 401(k) and other retirement plans require an employee to work at least a thousand hours in a year before being allowed to join. This rule often sidelines part-time workers averaging less than twenty hours a week. This is a perfect example of why you should review your SPD to see whether this rule applies to your plan. If it does, don't worry; you still may qualify based on your *actual* working hours. For example, if you have clocked overtime, you may exceed the thousand hours for the year and, if so, should be let into the plan. You may even be entitled to make up contributions owed for past oversights.

If your review indicates that your plan participation *was* improperly denied, don't fret. Your next move is to draft a straightforward letter to the plan administrator. The SPD will usually tell you where to go for help. Start by asking your plan administrator to explain why you are not allowed to participate. They should walk you through the SPD. If what they say makes sense, you at least know why you are not permitted in the plan. If you don't understand or think the administrator may have made a mistake, send another letter explaining why you should be admitted. For example, if you are a part-time employee, you might point out that your review of the SPD did not reveal any exclusion for part-time employees, nor did you see an hourly requirement. The plan is required to respond to your letter. In my experience, if you are correct, the plan should let you participate and take corrective measures for past issues. I've found that most plans try to administer the plan correctly and make corrections if required.

## CORRECTIVE MEASURES

Corrective measures vary based on the plan type. For instance, you would receive contributions missed during your exclusion period if you should have been participating in a profit-sharing plan. If the company contributes 5% of compensation each year and you earned $30,000, you would need to be reimbursed $1,500 (0.05 × $30,000) for being wrongfully excluded that year, plus interest.

The situation gets trickier to understand with a 401(k) plan. When an employee misses a chance to contribute to the plan, their salary is paid, but the employee or the employer makes no contributions. The employee has lost the opportunity to defer taxes on the portion of their salary that would have been contributed, so in this situation, the IRS requires that the plan sponsor (the company) correct the problem even though the employee was paid their salary. The corrective payment is generally 50% of the contribution the employee would have made if they had been included in the plan (although sometimes the 50% correction can be reduced to 25%). The employer must make this contribution on behalf of the employee based on the employee's compensation and the average contributions for all employees in the plan. In addition, the employee will also receive the employer's full matching contribution and be enrolled in the plan going forward.

Meet Donald, a part-time employee who earned $30,000 and was wrongly left out of his 401(k) plan. The plan provides a match equal to 100% of the first 3% of compensation contributed. On average, the company's employees contribute 5% of their compensation, which means Donald would have likely contributed about $1,500 ($30,000 × 0.05). The company would therefore make a corrective contribution equal to 50% of the contribution the employee would have made, or $750 ($30,000 × 0.05 × 50%). The company would also pay $900 in a corrective matching contribution ($30,000 × 0.03).

Keep in mind that Donald got paid his regular earnings through payroll. He lost the opportunity to defer taxes on a portion of his earnings by contributing some of his wages to the plan. In other words, Donald received the $750 (minus taxes) in this example through payroll, and it is now in his bank account; nevertheless, the employer has to spend *another* $750, in the form of a plan contribution (plus earnings based on IRS rules) to compensate Donald for the error. Some may view this as a windfall to the employee because he was paid the additional $750. Nevertheless, the IRS correction is required. In addition to recouping lost contributions, the employee now has the opportunity to participate going forward.

It can sometimes be challenging to prove that you were denied participation in a 401(k) because participation is voluntary, meaning you generally have to opt in to participate. In other words, the plan may advise that you were eligible to participate, but you never elected to opt in, resulting in your voluntary exclusion, and no corrections need to be made. You can always enroll at that point going forward. But if your plan *denies* you the opportunity to opt in, then that's a *mandatory exclusion* that needs to be rectified if it is improper. I always recommend that employees denied 401(k) participation check the SPD to determine whether the denial seems appropriate and, if not, send a letter to advise the administrator of your situation.

**If you were improperly denied participation, most plans will do the right thing and provide a corrective contribution to compensate for past errors and allow you to participate going forward.**

In another real-life example, a student intern was initially excluded from a plan due to his intern status, although he had received plan notices suggesting he could contribute. He successfully challenged this exclusion when a review of the SPD revealed no exclusions for interns or part-time employees or even an hourly requirement for eligibility. As a result, he was admitted to the plan.

If you have been excluded, don't worry. Help has arrived.

Due to a law change, 401(k) plans must allow contributions by employees with more than five hundred hours of service for three consecutive twelve-month periods, starting January 1, 2024. This changed to two consecutive twelve-month periods, taking effect on January 1, 2025.

## SUMMARY

- **If you are or were a part-time, seasonal, temporary, or similar type of employee and were advised that you are not eligible to participate in your company's retirement plan, request and review the SPD to determine whether you were improperly excluded.**
- **You might be entitled to participate in the plan, receive corrective contributions for past errors in your account, and participate in the plan going forward.**

# CHAPTER 16

## Problem Two—Is Your Compensation Calculation Wrong?

It is an unsettling realization, but there are more ways that companies can make mistakes with how much they put into your 401(k).[1] In addition to misinterpreting your eligibility based on employee status as full-time, part-time, or other, they sometimes misinterpret what constitutes "compensation." In fact, error number 3 on the IRS 401(k) Fix-It Guide covers improperly using the definition of compensation.[2] This mistake can happen if your company doesn't include *all* of your compensation in the calculation required by your plan terms, such as bonuses, overtime, or commissions. This means you could end up with less in your retirement account than you should have.

Most retirement plans, including 401(k)s and profit-sharing plans, use your compensation to determine your retirement benefits. For instance, in a 401(k), you might decide to save 10% of your compensation. However, what counts as "compensation"?

### PLAN CORRECTION

Carole, an IT specialist, participates in a 401(k) plan. She wants to save 10% of her compensation, and her plan says both her base salary and bonuses count as compensation. If her company *doesn't* count her bonus, they will deduct less from her paycheck when calculating *her* contributions, and they will also miscalculate the amount they owe her as an employer match. However, there is hope: The IRS has guidelines that require the company to fix this mistake, although it may not completely compensate for the shortfall.[3] Let's take a look.

If Carole earns $50,000 as a salary and receives a $6,000 bonus, her total compensation is $56,000. That means her company should withhold $5,000 from her regular paycheck, and $600 from her bonus paycheck, and contribute all those funds into Carole's 401(k) for a total contribution of $5,600 (0.1 × $50,000) + (0.1 × $6,000). However, if her company counts only her base salary and excludes the bonus, they will put only $5,000 (0.1 × $50,000) into the plan on her behalf. She will also receive her full bonus in cash of $6,000 because her contribution election on her bonus of $600 was not honored.

Since this is a common problem, the IRS has a correction for this error. But they require that only the employer deposit *50% of the contribution shortfall* (not 100%), which means $300 (0.5 × $600) credited to Carole's account in the plan. The end result is that she winds up receiving her full bonus of $6,000 in cash plus the correction for a total bonus essentially of $6,300. Some would call this a windfall for her, but she did miss the opportunity to invest those funds being tax-deferred in the plan, and the IRS recognizes this. This is confusing, so let's take a quick look at the math behind the correction step-by-step:

- Contribution to correct shortfall: $300 ($6,000 × 0.1 × 0.5)
  - » Cash bonus paid to Carole: $6,000
  - » Total received (bonus plus correction): $6,300

- Correct calculation with included bonus
  - » Total bonus that should be received (no error): $6,000 ($5,400 cash ($6,000 − $600) + $600 plan (0.1 × $6,000))

- Windfall to Carole: $300 ($6,300 − $6,000)

Let's now assume Carole is also entitled to a match. The match is a full match, up to 6% of compensation. However, if the bonus amount were excluded from compensation, she would receive a match of only $3,000 (0.06 × $50,000 salary and no bonus), where it should be $3,360 (0.06 × $56,000 salary and bonus), resulting in a shortfall of $360 ($3,360 – $3,000).

The IRS requires that the *employer match be corrected at 100%* rather than at 50% as in the case of an employee contribution correction. So upon making the adjustment, her employer would deposit an additional $360 into her account (0.06 × $6,000).

Profit-sharing plans can have the same problem. However, the correction method is different. In a profit-sharing plan, your company contributes a percentage of your income to your plan. In Giancarlo's company, the employer contribution should be 5% of his compensation (including base pay and bonus). Suppose his compensation is $50,000 in salary plus a $5,000 bonus. In that case, he should receive a $2,750 contribution ($55,000 × 0.05). But if his company forgets to include his bonus, his contribution will be $250 less than it should be $2,500 ($5,000 bonus × 0.05). Again, the IRS will require a *full* correction for the *employer* contribution of $250 for Giancarlo.

To sum it up, the IRS correction of 50% applies only to 401(k) *employee* contributions, not to matching contributions or profit-sharing plans, like the one in Giancarlo's example, which require 100% correction.

Although errors like these may sound trivial, they can add up over time, especially when considering the power of compounding. For example, a $250 shortfall each year for ten years at 4% interest (low interest rates used per IRS rules) results in over $3,000.

Knowing this, I spend a fair amount of my time looking at compensation when reviewing a plan for compliance problems. My reviews begin by interviewing the plan administrative staff. When focusing on compensation (a primary focus), I ask the team to walk me through the compensation used for 401(k) employees and matching contributions. During one review, several thousand employees had not received the contributions they were entitled to. The interview went something like this:

*Me: What compensation basis do you use for employee and matching contributions?*

*Them: All compensation.*

*Me: Does compensation include each person's bonus?*

*Them: No!*

They are wrong, and I know this because I have checked the plan rules. The definition of compensation states that salary *and* bonus should be included in compensation.

*Me: I am now very concerned. I checked the plan's records and found that the bonus was not included for retirement plan purposes, although it should have been.*

The result of this audit was that the plan was forced to correct this error through large make-up contributions to the accounts of thousands of employees. Of course, this was fixed going forward as well.

## HOW TO CHECK FOR COMPENSATION ERRORS—AND WHY BOTHER?

From my experience, most companies don't make these mistakes on purpose. If you bring it to their attention, they will likely fix it. That is why monitoring your payroll and retirement statements is so important. If you are proactive and informed, you can help ensure you get the full retirement benefits you deserve.

> **Remember: It is your money, your retirement, and your future. Make sure you are getting what is rightfully yours!**

Employer payroll systems are different from plan recordkeeping systems, and sometimes the communication between the two needs to be fixed. Manual (human) interventions can also cause accidental errors, such as causing the payroll system to send incorrect compensation data to the recordkeeping system. Below is a process outlined to help uncover mistakes.

First, request the latest copies of your pay slips, the SPD for your plan, and your latest 401(k) statement.

Second, review the SPD to see what counts as compensation. Does it include your salary only, salary plus bonus, or other items, like commissions and overtime pay? Knowing what is included is an important step.

Third, determine how much compensation you have chosen to contribute to your retirement plan, which is generally expressed as a percentage. This information is usually available in your plan's online portal.

Fourth, calculate how much should have been contributed to your plan based on your pay. For example, if you contribute 10% of your compensation of $40,000, you should see a contribution from each monthly paycheck of $333.33 ($40,000 × 0.1 ÷ 12) by the end of the year.

Finally, compare the calculated contribution to your pay stub. If they match or are very close, you are all set. If you need help, talk to your plan administrator.

If you are bonus eligible and the bonus is included in plan compensation, check your 401(k) contributions during normal and bonus pay periods. If the amount you contributed is different from what you expected to contribute, ask your plan for an explanation.

Let us say you decide to save 10% of your compensation, and your regular salary per pay period is $2,000. This means you should contribute $200 each pay period. However, if you receive a bonus of $5,000 in one pay period, your contribution should increase by $500 (0.10 × $5,000), totaling $700 in the pay period of the bonus.

If you find no issues, this checkup ensures you are on track to receive the full retirement benefits you were promised. You should try to do this in your first year, every five years or so, and after any major changes to your plan or its administration, such as a record-keeper change. Following these steps can help ensure your retirement savings are on track and allow you to catch any discrepancies early.

## SUMMARY

- **Compensation miscalculations are common, especially with bonuses, overtime pay, and commissions.**
- **The IRS has guidelines for how companies must**

correct these errors. The procedures to correct employee contributions and employer matches are different.

- Check your SPD and pay stubs periodically to be sure your company calculates compensation correctly.

# CHAPTER 17

## Problem Three—Are You Taking Your Distributions Too Late?

Required minimum distributions (RMDs) are an important component of retirement planning that is beneficial to learn about, even if retirement seems far off into the future. RMDs are minimum amounts that plan participants are required to withdraw from their 401(k) or IRA accounts once they reach a certain age, as determined by the Internal Revenue Code. At the time of this writing, that age is seventy-three, and it is projected to increase to seventy-five starting in 2033.

RMDs are not just something for plan participants to think about. They are also a consideration for people who inherit retirement accounts, regardless of the participant's age at death.

### EXPLORING RMDS WHEN YOU'RE STILL YOUNG

For many readers, this topic may not feel particularly relevant given that you may not have a clear picture of your future situation and finances. However, it's still worthwhile to understand how this fits into the bigger financial puzzle.

This brings back visions of my marathon days, thinking about the distant finish line while approaching the starting line. The thought was scary, but I quickly refocused on the steps ahead. In financial planning, understanding the basics can help you select the most appropriate strategies and accounts. But before we get into investment strategy, let's wrap our heads around what RMDs are and why they are so important.

Normally, you are required to withdraw money from your retirement account in the year you reach age seventy-three (or age seventy-five starting in 2033) unless you keep working. In that case, you may be able to delay the RMD until you retire, but not all plans allow this exception. The first RMD must be taken by the end of that year after you reach age seventy-three or seventy-five (if the exception does not apply), but you can delay this first withdrawal until April 1 of the following year. After that, RMDs must be taken by December 31 of each year. At the time you are required to withdraw, you can generally take your RMD in one lump sum, or you can choose to take it over your life expectancy if the plan allows it, which is generally preferable because taxes are deferred. If your plan does not allow lifetime payments, you can transfer your money to an IRA and withdraw the distributions from that account over your life or life expectancy.

So far, so good. The next thing to understand is that the amount of your RMD changes each year based on your age and the balance of your 401(k)s, IRAs, and other tax-deferred accounts as of December 31 of the previous year. The IRS has a uniform lifetime table showing ages at the end of the current year and corresponding distribution periods, which estimate the years you will take RMDs (which the IRS calls the *lifetime expectancy factor*). For example, if you are seventy-three, the IRS distribution period is 26.5 years, which means you can spread out your distributions over that length of time once you attain age seventy-three—but no longer. If, for example, you are or will turn seventy-three this year, and you have a 401(k) balance of $500,000 at December 31 of last year, your RMD for your first RMD year is about $18,868.

Good to know. But here's the catch, which is something you may not have to worry much about now but is something to keep in the back of your mind for someday: If your plan does not distribute the RMD as required, *you* will owe the taxman a significant penalty on top of your regular income taxes—*25% of the shortfall.* (This penalty was reduced from 50% after 2022, and the taxman is rumored to be in a horrible mood because of this reduction. When I think about this, it reminds me of an old Beatles song called "Taxman." The Beatles begin this classic by singing that you will receive one dollar for every $20 you earn, and the taxman will get $19. Why? Because of the *taxman*.)

Let's continue with the same example. If your regular income tax rate was 20%, and the IRS charged you a 25% penalty tax because you did not distribute your RMD, you would owe the IRS roughly $8,491 (0.45 × $18,868) versus the taxes you would have normally paid of $3,774 (0.20 × $18,868). So it literally "pays" to make sure your plan distributes the correct amount on time. If you do miss an RMD or are late in withdrawing it but correct the error within two years, the tax penalty can be reduced from 25% to 10%. You can also apply to the IRS for relief from the 25% or 10% penalty, using Form 5329, if the missed or late distribution was due to reasonable cause, with steps being taken to make up the distribution. Sometimes, your employer will help prepare this form. Either way, you should involve your tax professional with these issues. Even if you receive relief from the IRS, taking the RMD when it is due is much simpler. That way, you can avoid filing forms with the IRS and dealing with your employer on this issue.

Unfortunately, I've seen a lot of noncompliance in this area by plan administrators, including common mistakes like missed payout deadlines, which can trigger penalties even in large plans with well-recognized brands. The IRS has also seen this a lot and even has a web page, "Fixing Common Plan Mistakes—Failure to Timely Start Minimum Distributions," describing this as a common error.[1]

> **All this means that, yet again, it's important to understand your plan and monitor activity in your retirement accounts while you are working and after you retire.**

Now that you understand the basics and the risks of not taking those RMDs when required, we can explore how to manage your money now in anticipation of the future. One alternative is to design a diverse portfolio that includes Roth IRAs, which *do not require RMDs,* and Roth 401(k)s, which are *exempt from these rules* under the Internal Revenue Code. This would be a good choice if you want the flexibility to work part-time in retirement and therefore you prefer to contribute to accounts that offer more control over when to withdraw. Over the years, your Roth IRAs can grow tax-free, and you can delay distributions when you are still working, if you don't need them. It's never too early to start thinking about how to manage RMDs later!

One thing to note is that, although Roth 401(k)s are exempt from the Internal Revenue Code rules about RMDs, some Roth 401(k) plans may still require RMDs according to their specific terms. If yours does, you should consider rolling over the 401(k) account (or at least the Roth portion) to a Roth IRA before age seventy-three to avoid these distribution requirements. Similarly, if your 401(k) requires you to take a lump sum distribution rather than RMDs over your lifetime, you may wish to roll over your distribution to an IRA so that you can spread out your RMDs in a way that allows you to defer taxes for as long as possible.

## RMDS AND DEATH DISTRIBUTIONS

Seniors who have accumulated significant retirement assets in traditional IRAs or 401(k)s often have to deal with complicated RMD issues involving tax implications and estate planning. However, adult children of seniors, who may inherit these accounts, or any beneficiaries of an account owner who dies, may also have to face significant tax implications.

When a 401(k) or IRA owner dies, regardless of their age, the entire amount must generally be paid to a beneficiary within five years if there's no designated beneficiary or within ten years if there's a designated beneficiary. Account owners, therefore, should make sure to name a designated beneficiary (or beneficiaries) not only to be sure the correct beneficiaries inherit the money but also to take advantage of the ten-year rule and delay tax payments due. Note that the entire remaining account balance must be paid to the beneficiary (or beneficiaries) by December 31 of the tenth year after the owner's death. For example, if the owner died in 2025, the plan must fully distribute the IRA to the designated beneficiary by December 31, 2035. But the beneficiary is also required to take the RMDs during the years leading up to that date.[2] A 25% tax penalty applies to any shortfall if these distributions are not made. And, of course, the distributions are taxable to the beneficiaries at their regular income tax rates.

Several exceptions to the ten-year rule allow the payout to be stretched over the *beneficiary's* lifetime. These exceptions apply to spouses, a minor child, a disabled person, a chronically ill person, or someone not more than ten years younger than the account owner. For example, you can leave your account to your spouse to stretch the distributions over your joint lifetime; this will minimize taxes and help your account grow—free from income taxes—for a longer period. Also, rather than taking the full amount within ten years, the surviving spouse can choose to treat the inherited IRA as their own, which means they will begin to take the RMDs when *they* reach age seventy-three or seventy-five, as discussed above. This lets the assets grow for a longer time on a tax-free basis.

## PLANNING OPPORTUNITIES

The ten-year rule that requires nonspouse beneficiaries to take out RMDs and then the entire remaining balance within ten years can mean substantial tax liability. Roth accounts can help your beneficiaries by leaving them a more tax-efficient inheritance because the distributions are tax-free if the account was open for at least five years prior to the owner's death. This can be helpful if the adult child beneficiary is expected to be in a higher tax bracket than the parent when distributions are made. This will minimize tax liability and maximize the value of the inheritance. And even if a younger adult child is your beneficiary, a Roth conversion can help them because you paid taxes upfront upon conversion. By converting smaller amounts yearly and spreading the tax payments over several years, you may be paying taxes at a lower rate than your child would. This is particularly helpful if the parent does not need the funds for living and would rather let them grow tax-free.

These considerations are complicated and best applied in certain specific situations. I highlighted this topic so that it at least can be considered, as it can have a significant impact. Due to the intricacies, consulting with an accountant or other financial advisor is highly recommended. These professionals can help address your specific financial circumstances.

## SUMMARY

- RMDs will have a significant impact on your income after retirement, and strict rules must be followed to avoid costly tax consequences.
- Death distributions, which are minimum payouts imposed on beneficiaries when plan participants die, also have significant tax consequences for heirs.
- Roth conversions can help manage RMDs tax efficiently for participants and their beneficiaries.

# CHAPTER 18

## Problem Four—Are You Missing Out on Your Service Credit?

Frequent job changes have become normal in today's economy. Four million workers, or 2.5% of the workforce, changed employment every month in 2022.[1] This is equivalent to a 30% turnover rate over a full year! It's surprising for some people to learn that they might not be entitled to some or all of their matching contributions when changing jobs because they forfeited these funds by not having enough service.

This chapter examines the *service crediting rules* to help you understand how your length of service should be calculated and determine whether your plan's rules have been applied correctly in your case. These concepts will be especially valuable in the event you terminate your employment with a matching or profit-sharing account that is partially vested. A quick review might alert you to an error that could recover some money that you have legally earned, so investing a few minutes in this chapter might pay off.

### THE PURPOSE OF SERVICE CREDITING

Counting an employee's length of service is a fundamental requirement in retirement plan administration. Plans often use service crediting to determine eligibility, vesting, and benefit accrual (in a defined benefit plan). This appears to be a simple task, but the rules are tricky, and mistakes by plans are fairly common.

In a retirement plan such as a 401(k), vesting refers to the percentage of your account that you own, and amounts that are not vested may be forfeited by employees upon termination. The vesting schedule is found in the plan document and SPD. As seen in chapter 1, a common vesting schedule, known as *cliff vesting*, provides that an employee is 0% vested until three years of service, when they become 100% vested with no risk of forfeiture. Under this schedule, employees remain 0% vested after years one and two.

Compare this to immediate vesting or graded vesting. *Immediate vesting* means you own your employer-matching or profit-sharing contributions as soon as they are contributed. Your employee contributions are also 100% vested when made and can never be forfeited because they cannot be legally subject to a vesting schedule. In *graded vesting*, you are entitled to a larger percentage of your account each year you work until 100% is earned. Six-year graded vesting is popular, where an employee vests in 20% of the employer's contribution after two years of service and an additional 20% each following year until reaching 100% after six years.

Service crediting is also sometimes used to determine an employee's eligibility to participate in a plan. For instance, you may have to meet minimum age requirements, such as age twenty-one, or satisfy a service requirement, such as one year of service, to join a plan. ERISA, the federal law that applies to 401(k) plans, says that, in most cases, 401(k) plans cannot make you work for more than one year before you join. An exception to this is if the plan provides for immediate vesting, where you can be required to have worked for the company for two years before contributions commence. A 401(k) plan, on the other hand, cannot use the two-year rule for *your* contributions. However, a 401(k) plan with profit-sharing and matching contribution features can require two years of service before matching contributions and profit-sharing contributions start but only one year of service before your contributions begin. A plan can always establish more liberal or no service conditions.

## HOW SERVICE IS CREDITED AND ASSOCIATED PROBLEMS

Let's discuss various service crediting methods so that you understand the basics and flag some common issues that may apply. The SPD will describe the method used by your plan. Before we explore these methods, first we need to look at a common item: the *actual hours counted*. The employee should receive *credit for each hour worked* or is entitled to pay (vacation, holiday, illness, etc.), and a specific number of hours in a period is required to obtain credit. Most plans credit a year of service if one thousand hours are completed in twelve months. Under this method, service must be credited if an employee works less than twelve months but accumulates one thousand hours in a shorter period.[2] Knowing this, let's look at three common methods.

### *Potential Problem Alert—1,000-Hour Rule Incorrectly Applied*

In my experience, plans sometimes make mistakes in applying the 1,000-hour rule. In these cases, an employee works the hours required each year but does not complete the twelve months in their final year, and the plan erroneously does not provide credit for the year. This can affect your vesting in the match, if applicable.

For example, Victor is credited 40 hours per week and will accumulate 1,000 hours in twenty-five weeks (a little over six months). Assume Victor's plan requires three years to be 100% vested, with no vesting before attaining the three-year threshold. Victor leaves after two years and seven months, but he had accumulated at least 1,000 hours in the seven months and should receive credit for three years of service. If Victor did not receive a year of service credit for the seven months, vesting service would be inappropriately denied. This error could be the difference between zero vesting (receiving nothing) and full vesting (receiving his full match for three years). Victor should check his participant statement to confirm his vested amount before he terminates.

By understanding and monitoring your vesting calculations while you're still employed, you can save money and heartache after you leave.

*Elapsed time:* The employee should receive *credit for the time (elapsed)* between the start date and the termination date, regardless of the number of hours worked. Under this method, full-time *and* part-time employees eligible to work will get full credit for their service, regardless of hours worked.

For example, if an employee works from April 1, 2018, through March 31, 2020, two years of service will be credited because, under this method, two years have been worked from the date of employment through the date of termination. On the other hand, if the employee works from April 1, 2018, through January 1, 2020, less than two years will be credited (one year and nine months).

## Potential Problem Alert—Elapsed Time Rule Not Applied

I have seen mistakes in applying the elapsed time rules. Sometimes, the plan document requires the *elapsed time* method, but the plan administrator does not use this method in practice. Instead, the *actual hours* method described earlier is used, which is incorrect. This error can wrongfully delay or even deny participation and vesting, but it is straightforward to check. If your SPD requires the elapsed time method, you should confirm that the plan does not count hours, particularly if you are not vested.

Let us consider Greg's plan. His SPD stated that the elapsed time method would be used to credit service for vesting purposes, and the matching contributions had a three-year cliff vesting schedule. Greg worked ten hours a week from January 1, 2020, through December 31, 2022, and received three full years of credited service under the elapsed time method and was fully vested in his matching contributions when he left.

However, if his plan had improperly used the *actual hours* crediting method rather than the *elapsed time* method to credit his service, Greg would not have been vested. Under the actual hours counting method, the match would have been forfeited because he only worked 520 hours (10 × 52) per year over each of the three years rather than 1,000 hours in any plan year. He would have been denied his match because the wrong service crediting method was used. Ouch!

Consider another situation where Rita's plan required a year of service before she could participate, and the plan incorrectly used the actual hours method instead of the required elapsed time method. Under the actual hours method, she needed to complete 1,000 hours of service in a plan year before she could join, but she worked only 80 hours a month, or 960 hours in twelve months. She fell short and never became eligible. If the plan had used the correct elapsed time method, she would have entered the plan after completing a year of service and been allowed to participate in employee contributions without regard to the number of hours.

*Equivalency:* This method combines the actual hours and the elapsed time methods by crediting the employee with a set number of hours for each period worked, regardless of the actual hours worked. For example, they may be credited with 10 hours for every day worked, 45 hours for every week worked, 95 hours for every semimonthly pay period, or 190 hours for each month worked.

## Potential Problem Alert—Equivalency Rule Not Applied

Meet Juancho, whose SPD requires the use of the monthly equivalency method, where if Juancho performs *any service* in a month, he should be treated as working 190 hours that month. The matching contributions have a three-year vesting requirement (cliff vesting), which means he needs 1,000 hours in twelve months to receive credit for a year of service. Assume he works 80 hours monthly from January 1, 2020, through December 31, 2022, or 960 hours per year (12 × 80). However, the plan mistakenly uses the *actual hours* method rather than the *equivalency* method, so they deem his hours insufficient by 40 hours to be eligible. He receives no credit and forfeits the match. However, under the correct 190-hour monthly *equivalency* method, Juancho should have received 190 hours for each month he worked. Therefore, for each full year, he would have been credited with 2,280 hours (12 × 190). This far exceeds the 1,000 hours required, and Juancho would have earned a year of service for each year worked and been fully vested in his matching contributions when he left the company. That hurts! Juancho was entitled to and should receive the match, provided he uncovers this issue and notifies his plan administrator or human resources department.

The lesson: Check your SPD to be sure you understand your

service crediting policy and verify that you are being properly credited for your service.

## REHIRES OR BREAKS IN SERVICE

You may be fortunate to receive proper crediting while you work and after employment is terminated. But then what happens if the company rehires you?

Many problems can arise when employees leave and are rehired. If this applies to you, review your SPD regarding these rules, particularly if you are not vested in some or all of your benefits. Generally, your service credits should *not* be affected if you are rehired by your company *within five consecutive years* of termination. However, there are instances where the previous service is incorrectly disregarded by the plan administrator, and they treat you like a new employee with no service because these rules are misapplied. If this situation is applicable to you, review your SPD for more information on the break-in-service rules to ensure your service credits are correctly applied to your vesting and participation.

## TIPS TO STAY ON TOP OF YOUR SERVICE CREDITS

This is a lot to digest, so here are some simple steps to help you do your best:

1. Keep track of your employment start and end dates with your employer.
2. Verify the service crediting method provided in your SPD: actual hours, elapsed time, or equivalency.
3. Determine how many years and months you have worked or service hours you should have earned and your vesting date. Ask your administrator to confirm your vesting date. If you have never been rehired and are a full-time employee, determine how many years and months of service you have accumulated between your employment

start and end dates. This should give you a reasonable estimate of the service you have earned. Review the common errors above and make sure they do not apply to you.

4. If you find discrepancies between your estimates and the plan records, contact the plan administrator and request an explanation of how your service was determined.

## SUMMARY

- **Service credits may be applied using the actual hours, elapsed time, or equivalency methods.**
- **Administrators often make mistakes when calculating credits.**
- **If you have been rehired, worked part-time, changed your hourly status, or moved within the company, watch for vesting miscalculations and ask for help if you are close to being vested. Obtain confirmation when you are fully vested.**

# CHAPTER 19

## Problem Five—Contribution Elections, Automatic Enrollment, and Automatic Escalation Sometimes Go South

A friend recently told me a joke about a taxi ride in New York City, which brought to mind some of my experiences in the city that apply to this chapter. Mun (pronounced *moon*) hailed a taxi in NYC, explaining to the driver that he was in a rush. The cab driver assured him not to worry and started driving incredibly fast, like a bat flying out of hell. The driver sped up even more as they approached an intersection with a yellow light and barreled through. Mun was convinced at this point that he was going to die.

"Please slow down and be careful; you just sped through a yellow light," Mun said.

The driver responded, "In this city, yellow lights mean speed up, so don't worry so much. My fellow cabbies taught me this NYC rule, and we all drive like this."

Next, they approached a red light, and Mun assumed the driver would surely stop. Nevertheless, he slowed down briefly and then sped right on through. Panic surged through Mun as he held on to the edge of his seat. He yelled, "Please drive more carefully or let me out."

"Don't worry so much," the driver responded. "My friends and I have been driving this way for many years, and it has always been fine."

When they got close to a green light, the driver stopped for no reason.

Mun asked, "Why did you stop at a green light?" He was confused yet relieved at the same time.

The driver replied, "I need to be very careful because one of my buddies could be driving on the other street."

In this driver's world, green means stop, yellow means speed up, and red is optional. In the context of a 401(k) plan, some plans treat your choices, also called *elections*, as if they were optional red lights. Sometimes, your Roth elections (first mistake) and automatic enrollment provisions (second mistake) are followed, but sometimes, they are not.

The first mistake is so common that it appears prominently on the IRS web page "Fixing Common Mistakes—Correcting a Roth Contribution Failure."[1] It involves the plan not honoring the participant's Roth election and mistakenly treating the contribution as a traditional one. The second mistake is found in automatic enrollment plans that mistakenly enroll only employees who affirmatively elect to enroll instead of automatically enrolling them unless they opt out, as stated by the plan terms. The IRS addresses this mistake and shows how to correct it.[2] Mistakes such as these, which we explore in depth below, can be caused by various reasons, such as when manual intervention is built into the administrative process. After reading this chapter, you should be able to easily spot these issues and ensure that, if they apply to you, they can be promptly and correctly addressed.


## ROTH ELECTIONS

Many 401(k) plans offer Roth contributions, which are made after taxes and allow for tax-free and penalty-free income and distributions provided at least five years have passed between the participant's first Roth contribution and the distribution. No taxes are due at the withdrawal time because Uncle Sam has already been paid. (On the other hand, traditional 401(k) plan contributions offer tax-deductible contributions and tax-free income until distributions are made. See chapter 6 for more information on Roth contributions, including circumstances when they should be used.) According to the 66th Annual Survey, 99% of 401(k) plans offer a Roth feature, which means there is a good chance your plan offers this option.[3]

Let's take a closer look at mistakes made by plans allowing participants to choose between traditional and Roth contributions. Sometimes, the participant elects a Roth contribution, but the plan processes it as a pre-tax (traditional) contribution. Sometimes, the reverse happens, and the participant elects a pre-tax contribution, but the plan processes it as a Roth contribution. Below are two examples.

Eugene elected to defer 10% of his compensation into the 401(k) plan as a Roth contribution, but the employer (or plan administrator) records it as a traditional contribution. As a result, Eugene's year-end W-2 shows less taxable income than he should have, and he winds up paying less tax than he would have. This means that Eugene will ultimately be taxed when he withdraws from his account, whereas he would pay no tax on withdrawal if the Roth contribution were recorded correctly. This mistake adversely affects his financial planning if not addressed.

The plan can fix the problem under IRS rules by transferring the pre-tax contributions (i.e., the contributions coming from compensation that had never been taxed), along with related earnings, to Eugene's Roth account. However, this can lead to Eugene filing amended tax returns and paying unanticipated additional income taxes if the problem is discovered in a later tax year. He could have avoided this headache by checking his payroll records, which can usually be accessed online, during the plan year to ensure his Roth election was correctly honored when it was first made.

Serena had the opposite problem. She elected to defer 10% of her compensation into the 401(k) plan as a traditional contribution, meaning she would not have owed taxes on that portion of her compensation that year. However, the plan mistakenly treated the contribution as a Roth contribution, thus not following her election. As a result, Serena's year-end W-2 shows taxable income higher than it should have, and she wound up paying more tax than she should have in the year of contribution. She will also ultimately not be taxed when she withdraws from her account, whereas she would have paid tax on withdrawal if the traditional contribution were recorded correctly.

The plan can fix the problem by transferring the Roth contributions, with earnings, to the pre-tax contribution account. However, if the problem is discovered in a later tax year, this could lead to amended tax returns for Serena just as it did for Eugene. To catch this problem as soon as possible, Serena should have checked the payroll records from her employer to make sure that her pre-tax election was honored when it was first made.

## AUTOMATIC ENROLLMENT

The automatic enrollment feature in 401(k) plans was designed to help Americans save for retirement. The goal was to ensure that employees participate unless they take the initiative to opt out, and it has significantly increased participation for all employees, and particularly for Black, Latino, and lower-wage employees. This optional feature is typical; many employers have added or enhanced it, providing, for example, that each eligible employee is automatically enrolled to participate at 3% of their salary (the default percentage) unless the employee declines participation. Of course, one can always affirmatively participate at a different level (higher or lower).

There are two main issues with automatic features. First, the automatic feature default percentage might need to be set higher to enable you to meet your retirement needs. This is why automatic enrollment is not listed as an opportunity in part 2. Your savings under this program can be suboptimal, and you can generally do better by managing your enrollment levels on your own.

The second problem is that employers sometimes fail to add you to the plan even though enrollment is theoretically automatic. Let's look at an example of this.

Wendy's plan provides a six-month eligibility requirement. This means that once she has accumulated six months of required service, she will participate in the plan at the beginning of the first day of the following month. Wendy is given a notice before her eligibility date stating that she will automatically be enrolled at 3% unless she opts out of participation. She does not decline participation. But one year later, Wendy realizes that neither her employee contributions nor the company-matching contributions have been made.

As a result of this error, Wendy is entitled to corrective contributions. She will also be entitled to lost matching contributions provided by her plan and related earnings. The IRS realizes that employers make these types of mistakes and requires that the employer contribute 25% of the missed employee contribution, with related earnings, plus matching contributions if applicable. Note that the 25% corrective contribution for missed employee contributions does not apply if the plan corrects this within nine and a half months after the plan year in which the error occurred.

Wendy has a salary of $100,000 per year, and the error was corrected by Wendy's employer at the end of December *after* the year it occurred—more than the nine-and-a-half-month grace period. If the match were 3%, Wendy would be entitled to $3,000 ($100,000 × 0.03) plus earnings. In addition, she would be entitled to a corrective contribution, on her behalf, from her employer, amounting to $750 (0.03 × $100,000 × 0.25). Therefore, her total correction was $3,750.

When you enroll in a plan, you should always request and review a copy of the SPD to determine whether your plan provides for automatic enrollment. You should have also received a notice explaining this feature. If it does, and you do not decline participation, you should check your payroll records to ensure the required contribution is being withheld beginning on the correct date based on the SPD's eligibility provisions. If the contributions started late or were never made, you may be entitled to some additional corrective contributions and, of course, should be participating going forward.

One final point is worth mentioning. An employer's choice to add or enhance automatic enrollment has historically been voluntary. But starting in 2025, companies with *newly established* 401(k) plans (those established after 2022) must automatically enroll their employees at a minimum contribution rate of 3%, but no more than 10%. This maximum rate will increase by one percentage point each year up to 15%. Employees are not forced to enroll automatically at the default level, and they can always opt out. These required rules have exceptions for plans maintained by some small businesses.

## AUTOMATIC ESCALATION

Another potentially problematic automatic feature is automatic in-creases in contribution rates (sometimes called *automatic escalation*). Many plans have adopted an optional automatic escalation feature where the participant's initial contribution is automatically increased unless the participant opts out of the automatic increase. These in-creases are typically done annually. A plan might provide, for exam-ple, that any participant contributing at a rate less than 15% of pay shall automatically be increased by 1% each year until they reach the 15% threshold. If you are participating at the rate of 1% of pay at the beginning of year 1, you will be increased by 1% to a total of 2% auto-matically at the end of year 1. Although the plan administrator may very well be handling this process correctly, this feature can become a problem when you notice your take-home pay shrinking. Of course, you can always opt out of the automatic escalation increase or manu-ally set it. On the other hand, the default levels are often set too low, resulting in suboptimal savings. You can generally do better by man-aging these critical features independently.

Lastly, automatic escalation features can be problematic when the percentage is inadvertently *not increased* as the plan requires. You may assume your contribution is going up when, in fact, it is not. Again, you should obtain your plan's SPD to see if your plan provides automatic escalation. If it does, and you have not elected to decline this feature, you should review your plan's default percentage to en-sure it increases appropriately each year if the plan provides for this increase. You may be entitled to additional corrective contributions and related matching contributions if it has not been increasing in accordance with the plan.

> **Although automatic features are intended to help you manage your savings, they sometimes do not automatically operate as they should. It is up to you to verify they are working in your best interests.**

# SUMMARY

- Plan mistakes in processing Roth elections occur too often.
- Automatic enrollment and escalation features may not necessarily help you optimize your savings.
- Plan administrators can make mistakes in implementing automatic features.
- When plans make these types of errors, corrective measures are available, but participants can experience unnecessary headaches and costly tax or other financial consequences.

# CHAPTER 20

## Problem Six—What About Changes in Your Plan Administration or Corporate Structure?

Elon Musk's $44 billion deal to acquire Twitter (now X) and Heinz Company and Kraft Foods' $100 billion deal to create the new Kraft Heinz Company are examples of large mergers and acquisitions (M&As). These types of corporate events often affect employees by changing their roles, shaking up their reporting relationships, and modifying employee benefits, such as 401(k) plans and administration.

During my career at Mercer, I often helped organizations redesign retirement plans following an M&A transaction. In one case, around fifty companies merged to form a single company. Most of these companies had an existing 401(k) plan covering employees. We were retained to design one new plan for the entire organization. Ultimately, this meant that the plan of each company was substantially changed, and these changes had to be carefully explained to each employee so they understood their new options and were able to make important decisions about participation, investment selection, and beneficiary designation.

This plan redesign was accompanied by changes to the main

recordkeepers (e.g., Vanguard or another party) and payroll provider. Assets had to be transferred to the new plan, and other needed adjustments were made. There was a lot going on. The redesign streamlined the plan and simplified the administration but involved many moving parts, as is common in these transactions where transition to a new plan can lead to errors in plan administration. Similarly, when recordkeeper or payroll changes occur, errors in plan administration are more likely. This chapter aims to provide background information and practical guidance to help detect and avoid these errors.

## MERGERS AND ACQUISITIONS

M&As are significant transactions where two companies unite to form a single entity (merger) or one company purchases another (acquisition). These transactions aim to create synergy, thereby increasing the combined company's value beyond the sum of the separate entities. M&A transactions often impact the retirement plans sponsored by one or more companies. This can look like one of these examples:

- If only one of the companies had a plan before the merger, the newly formed company might take over as the plan sponsor and extend its coverage to all employees, including those who previously worked for the company without a plan. Other significant plan changes are also typical in such cases.
- If both companies had plans before the merger, these might be combined and unified, resulting in a single plan for the newly merged company. This new plan often undergoes significant revisions, like changes in the matching formula.
- One or both companies may decide to freeze or terminate their retirement plan(s), leading to a new plan for the newly formed company or, in some cases, complete elimination of this benefit.

Your company will inform you if the plan changes post-M&A. It is crucial to pay close attention to understand how the merger or acquisition will affect your 401(k) or pension. Plans often remain unchanged for about a year post-M&A, followed by significant changes.

## RECORDKEEPING CHANGES

Recordkeepers can be fund companies like Fidelity or Vanguard, insurance companies like Prudential or John Hancock, or payroll companies like ADP. (Some companies have an in-house payroll function, but most outsource some payroll functions to third parties.) Given their broad responsibilities, changes in recordkeepers need to be closely monitored, and plans, especially larger ones, routinely assess recordkeeper performance. Therefore, recordkeeper changes in a 401(k) plan are a common occurrence.

401(k) recordkeepers perform several plan-related tasks, including but not limited to the following:

- Managing employee enrollment
- Tracking employee investments
- Processing 401(k) hardship distributions and loans
- Preparing and distributing account statements to participants
- Handling compensation-related issues
- Providing phone support for participants
- Managing eligibility, vesting, and service-related issues

## THE PROBLEM WITH ADMINISTRATIVE CHANGES

When significant changes occur all at once under time pressure, things can sometimes go wrong. For example, if the plan is redesigned and the matching formula and compensation definitions are changed, plan processes and procedures need to be revised. A change in the compensation definition, from only salary to pay that includes bonus and overtime, would necessitate feeding changes to the plan's recordkeeping system. Furthermore, if there is manual intervention, such as coding the compensation as bonus or overtime, additional problems can arise. To sum it up, anytime things change, errors are more likely to occur.

Whenever a change in recordkeeper occurs, whether because of an M&A or for other reasons, plan administration is impacted. Participants are notified of these changes, which is why reviewing these notices and your statements following the change is critical.

## TIPS TO HELP MANAGE M&A CHANGES EFFICIENTLY

The following approach can help detect errors quickly, facilitating prompt and efficient resolution:

- Pay close attention to, and thoroughly review and understand, all the notices you receive describing important plan changes, such as matching contribution changes or changes in recordkeeping responsibilities in connection with an M&A transaction. You may also receive a summary of material modifications, which plan sponsors will provide so you have adequate time to respond to the changes in a timely manner. For example, suppose they change their investments due to a recordkeeping change. In that case, you may get a blackout notice if there is a blackout period during which you can't direct or diversify your accounts, take out loans, arrange for withdrawals, and so on.
- Review several participant account statements following the changes to ensure their reasonableness. Pay special attention to the accuracy in the compensation used (see chapter 16), service credit measurement if you are not already vested (see chapter 18), and the company match calculation (see chapter 7).
- Make sure your beneficiary designation forms are in good order.

If you identify issues, contact your plan administrator promptly, in writing. You may also want to refer to appendix B for how to get help if necessary. By following these steps and paying close attention to the details, you can ensure that changes in plan administration do not negatively affect your retirement security.

## SUMMARY

- **Changes in the plan recordkeeper or corporate structure, especially following an M&A transaction, can significantly affect your 401(k) plan and lead to errors.**
- **Pay close attention to plan notices and other documents provided to you when these changes occur as well as to your participant statements of account to identify any errors or other issues promptly.**

# CHAPTER 21

## Problem Seven—Contribute, Contribute, Contribute—but Is It Too Much?

Throughout this book, I have encouraged you to scrimp, save, and contribute. Some, or probably many, of you may accuse me of sounding like a broken record—contribute, contribute, contribute. But the record is not broken. It is fine—with the following caveat: Don't contribute too much.

As you know, the 401(k) contribution limit in 2024 was $23,000 for employee contributions (Roth or traditional) or $30,500 if you are fifty or older. This limit is an *individual limit*, not a plan limit, so you must combine *all* contributions made to *all* the 401(k) plans you participated in during the tax year to determine your total contribution. That means that if you worked for two different employers in 2024, each with a 401(k) plan, you could contribute only $23,000 in total—not $23,000 to each plan. (This limit does not apply to your matching contributions.)

For example, Amit is under age fifty and has two jobs offering 401(k) participation. Amit decides to participate in both. He is limited to the $23,000 annual limit, and he can split the contribution equally and contribute $11,500 to each plan. Or he can choose to split his maximum contribution limit in any manner between the plans so long as his total contributions made under both plans do not exceed $23,000.

## THE TAXMAN IS WATCHING

Employees often run into the problem of overcontributing when they change jobs. For example, when Richard moved from Google to Apple during 2024, he had already contributed $18,500 to his Google 401(k) plan. That left only $4,500 to contribute to his Apple plan, and he can contribute this amount on either a Roth or traditional basis. However, Richard needs to be careful because if he contributes too much, he may be subject to double tax on the overpayment.

First, the overpayment is included in his taxable income for the year contributed, and then it is taxed again when the contributions are ultimately distributed from the plan. Ouch! Double tax is always a bitter pill to swallow. The good news is that rectifying or avoiding the problem in the first place can be easy.

**Overcontributions can be costly and *taxed twice*.**

Most 401(k) plans have administrative procedures to prevent over-contributions, so the plan generally catches them. In the case of dual participation, however, neither 401(k) plan knows about the employee's participation in the other plan and thus can't prevent overcontribution. This responsibility falls on you. As the old adage goes, "With opportunity comes responsibility."

If an error is made, contact your plan administrator and ask for any excess contributions, along with any earnings accrued on these contributions, to be returned to you *by April 15* of the year following the one in which the contributions were erroneously made. You will also receive an amended W-2 form that includes this additional income, which you must report on your tax return for the year the over-contribution occurred. If you do not report the excess, the taxman will relish the chance to collect his double tax.

# SUMMARY

- Aim to contribute as much as possible, but ensure you do not exceed the annual maximum.
- Pay close attention to your contribution level and limits if you change 401(k) plans during the year.
- Request any excess contributions and earnings to be returned by April 15 of the year following the year the excess was contributed.

# CHAPTER 22

## Problem Eight—Does My Pension Plan Owe Me Money?

Golfing at Pebble Beach? Skiing in Patagonia? Cooking classes in Paris? Spotting mistakes in your defined benefit plan could bring you closer to this dream. If you are lucky enough to participate or have participated in this type of plan, double-check for common errors that, once fixed, could significantly boost your retirement savings. Defined benefit pension plans have been decreasing in popularity in the United States for years, and most companies have either terminated them or "frozen" them (stopped them from providing future benefits). Nevertheless, the potential for significant financial problems leads me to include them in this chapter for those lucky readers covered by these arrangements. And while you may be a number of years away from retirement, these issues surrounding defined benefit plans are something you should be aware of as you progress through your career if you have ever worked for an employer offering this retirement benefit.

If you do not participate in a defined benefit pension plan (and never have), go ahead and skip this chapter, as this information is irrelevant to you.

## DELAYED BENEFITS

*Defined benefit pension plans* are designed to pay benefits at the normal retirement age, which in most plans is sixty-five. Participants in these plans earn a benefit payable as an annuity for their life beginning at that point in time. However, plans generally do not pay benefits if participants are still employed after their normal retirement age; they wait until the participants retire. If you are part of a defined benefit pension plan and are working past normal retirement age at that employer (or did in the past), you may be entitled to *significant additional benefits*. This could happen if you do not receive a *suspension of benefits notice* at age sixty-five, which tells you that you can retire and start receiving your pension or keep working and delay the start of these benefits until retirement.[1]

Here is an example. Alison, age sixty-five, is entitled to a $2,000-a-month pension for the rest of her life. She chooses to keep working and delay the start of her pension until retirement. The plan was frozen (as are most plans today), meaning that Alison is not earning any additional benefits under the plan, but of course she is entitled to her previously earned $2,000-a-month pension. If she were to retire now, she could start her monthly retirement immediately. However, she does not plan to retire until age sixty-nine, and she will start her pension of $2,000 per month then.

Fast forward by four years. Alison is now sixty-nine, and her pension was unpaid for the four years since she turned sixty-five and while she was still employed. Those missed payments (excluding interest) total $96,000 ($2,000 × 12 months × 4 years). This significant amount, if not paid, can have a substantial impact on Alison's retirement plans. It is legal for the plan never to make the payments *if it provided Alison with a suspension of benefits notice during the month she turned sixty-five*. If this notice was *not* provided, Alison would be legally entitled to receive the $96,000, with interest, because the required information was not provided even though she had decided to keep on working.

The suspension of benefits notice should contain information like the general terms of the plan related to payment suspension for employees who keep working and a copy of the suspension terms. This rule is unique to defined benefit pension plans and does not apply to

401(k), profit-sharing, or other plans. Based on my experience, significant noncompliance in this area is very common and leads to costly corrections for plans. The IRS has long recognized this issue. If you are part of a defined benefit plan and think you are affected, contact your plan administrator for clarification. If you get denied or the response needs clarification, seek professional help because the stakes can be high.

There is a similar problem for those who leave their job before the normal retirement age but start their pensions after their normal retirement date. Generally, the benefits paid should be higher, which means the person is entitled to additional benefits.[2]

Jeremy left his job at fifty-two but had earned a pension of $1,500 per month from his previous employer, payable beginning at age sixty-five (normal retirement date). He didn't actually retire from his second employer, however, until age sixty-eight when he filed for pension benefits from the first employer. In this case, his monthly pension benefits should be increased to account for the delay in starting payments after the plan's normal retirement date, reflecting his older age and the shorter expected payout period. Therefore, Jeremy should have received $1,800 monthly at age sixty-eight, not $1,500. However, the plan did not adjust for the late start. The plan must adjust Jeremy's benefit to $1,800 monthly (based on his age when he started drawing the benefits) plus interest. Why, you might ask, would a participant leave his job and not begin his pension when he can? This could occur for a variety of reasons. In Jeremy's case, it is likely the employer simply failed to contact him when he was eligible to begin receiving benefits, although they were not obligated to issue a suspension of benefits notice since he was no longer working for them. It could be that Jeremy simply forgot.

So if this relates to you, be proactive and contact your plan administrator if you think you are entitled to significant additional amounts.

Mistakes also occur when the data is not correct. For example, incorrect birth dates can affect start dates if the plan doesn't correctly calculate when you turn sixty-five. Benefit amounts would also be impacted by errors in such basic data. Your plan must have accurate information about your age, marital status, and years of employment. If not, you should inform your plan as soon as possible.

**The lesson to keep in mind is this: Defined benefit
pensions, including those sponsored by world-
class companies, sometimes don't provide the suspension of benefit notice and do not always adjust
to compensate for late retirement. Beware of these
issues as they can be significant. Also check your
personal information for accuracy.**

Congratulations to the fortunate few who have earned a defined
benefit plan. This will help significantly in your retirement. Since this
benefit is rare, I will not cover other common problems that can cause
the loss of your hard-earned promised benefit, including tricky rules
pertaining to *cash balance* pension plans.

## SUMMARY

- **If you ever participated in a defined benefit pension plan and are planning to delay your retirement,
whether at the original employer with the plan or another employer, pay close attention to your suspension
of benefits notice and benefit calculations.**

# PART IV

Tales and Conclusion

# CHAPTER 23

## Real-Life Examples of Success and Failure

In researching individual savings rates, I found many examples of people saving 25% or more of their sometimes modest income. One example was a couple, both teachers, who started making $48,000 combined, with one spouse working part-time. This is about $85,000 in today's dollars, assuming a 4% yearly raise.[1] They lived in a small apartment with a mortgage payment of about $350 per month and kept their total expenses under $20,000 annually. Their salaries generally increased over time. They supplemented their income with tutoring and other education-based activities, and the part-time spouse became full-time. They saved significant portions of their combined salaries, sometimes saving $40,000 per year or even more. They retired before age thirty.

Saving large percentages of earnings by keeping expenses very low is difficult and depends on individual circumstances. Personal obligations, like raising children or helping support your parents, can further complicate this. Other factors, such as geography, can also have a significant effect. For example, New York City offers many high-paying job opportunities, yet the cost of living is sky-high and can make saving a huge challenge. Other cities and rural areas have a lower cost of living, so each dollar buys more. This couple had adopted a frugal lifestyle and were part of a financial independence, retire early (FIRE) movement.

The FIRE movement's foundation is based on a simple principle: Save a significant portion of your income, often suggested to be 50% or more, and invest it wisely in a diversified portfolio of assets. The goal is to build a substantial nest egg to generate enough income to support a withdrawal rate, usually 4% annually, to fund your lifestyle without spending the principal.

Followers often embrace frugality to reduce living expenses. While reducing expenses is one side of the equation, increasing income is the other. This can involve career advancement, starting a side business, or investing in income-producing assets. The goal is to increase the gap between income and expenses to invest more toward financial independence.

The FIRE movement favors smart investing and prefers low-cost index funds or other passive income sources. This strategy is designed to grow wealth steadily over time, consistent with many of the principles discussed in this book. It focuses on long-term growth and compound interest rather than trying to beat the market through active trading.

Financial independence is not just about the numbers. It could mean retiring early to explore the world, pursuing a passion project without worrying about income, or even working part-time in a fulfilling career. The FIRE movement provides the tools and strategies to achieve this freedom, allowing you to pursue a life consistent with your values and aspirations.

As I started thinking about and researching this lifestyle, it became clear to me that it is not for everyone. Although I found story after story that resonated with me, I also realized that the sacrifice required for a 50% savings rate seemed rather extreme. There might be a middle ground better suited for many people. Ultimately, it would be best to decide what's most appropriate for you and your family.

Here is the story of a couple who gave up the FIRE lifestyle. At first, Michelle and Ernie eliminated virtually all activities that brought them joy.[2] They discontinued their cable subscription, reduced their cell phone data package, stopped dining out, and ceased weekly coffee outings. Everything that could be cut was because the prospect of early retirement justified these sacrifices for them. Or that is what they thought. But as their wealth increased, their contentment dropped significantly. Watching cable TV at night, enjoying Friday pizza nights, and going on Sunday coffee outings had all been sources of happiness for them. As time passed, the effects of significant savings became more unbearable.

Many individuals have ventured into early retirement only to confront unexpected challenges. Although Michelle and Ernie could have gone down this path, Michelle also recognized that she was in a fortunate position with good benefits from her job. She was nervous about giving up this stability to live a frugal existence reliant on savings, especially given the unpredictability of the future. Ultimately, they realized that this lifestyle was not for them, and enduring severe budgetary constraints to save for rapid retirement became untenable. When weighed against the benefits and the overall uncertainty about what the future might bring, the potential perils of a FIRE approach did not justify the pursuit.

They shifted their goals, aiming for financial security at a more gradual and enjoyable rate. Although they reached their financial retirement targets well before the usual retirement age, they decided not to leave their jobs. Instead, they love the idea of financial freedom without the need to deplete savings. Abandoning the early retirement goal has been liberating for them, allowing them to once again indulge in the pleasures of TV, pizza, and coffee. They came to build a fulfilling lifestyle through a more balanced financial strategy and smart financial decisions.

This gradual approach appeals to me, especially if it includes meaningful, secure work that is defined by not only financial benefits but also how it matches and supports one's values. Instead of *working to retire* (or quit), the philosophy is *working to improve life* (or thrive). Teachers, healthcare professionals, social workers, and public service professionals are examples of people who choose careers that are valued not solely for their contribution to society but also for the intrinsic satisfaction they bring. Many of these professions also provide great benefits, such as healthcare, retirement, and vacation time.

You must try your best to carefully research all possible opportunities to ensure a good fit and a healthy balance between financial health and life satisfaction. Ultimately, the choice is yours; whatever you choose, enjoy the journey!

## JOE'S STORY

When I think about a meaningful career, a friend of mine comes to mind. Joe, a beloved tennis teaching professional, dedicated his life to the game he loved and its players, leaving a meaningful impact on those who knew him. Even though he worked long hours, often clocking sixty to seventy hours a week, he found incredible meaning and happiness in his career, displaying passion and commitment. His career was dedicated to the sport he loved and every individual he coached. He took a personal interest in his students, not just as athletes but as people with dreams, fears, and aspirations. He attended their tournaments, formed close relationships with their parents, and was involved in their personal and athletic growth, with ties well beyond the tennis court.

Joe's enthusiasm for tennis was not only focused on the kids. He organized weekly clinics for adults, which quickly became the week's highlight for many participants. These sessions were great for honing skills, but they were also about building a group of players at all levels that shared a love for the game. Joe took great pride in this, creating a supportive and enjoyable environment focused not only on tennis but also on friendship, fun, and a shared passion that united people. And Joe was not just a tennis professional but a true family man. His wife and two sons obviously deeply loved him. He would sometimes talk to me about his visits with his mother. His ability to balance a demanding career with a close-knit family life was nice to see. He lived life fully and seemed to love every moment.

His untimely passing in his fifties was a significant loss to all who knew him. At his funeral, held in a large church in New Jersey, the sheer volume of attendees was proof of his impact. The church was packed, with several hundred mourners to pay their respects. The huge turnout, including some familiar faces and some new, was a testament to the many lives Joe had touched. The emotion and sadness at the ceremony was obvious, especially for me when my daughter, who adored Joe, started crying, moved by the loss of such a significant figure in her life.

Joe's legacy was clear then—his life was a mixture of worthy pursuits from dedication to his family, career, and community. It showed how finding meaningful work can transform hard work into a joyful and meaningful undertaking. His willingness to work long hours was not a burden but a source of satisfaction, as he was passionate about mentoring his students on and off the court. Joe enjoyed his hard work, which was on full display as he continued his daily routine, year after year, showing that when you do what you love, it does not feel like work.

Moreover, Joe was prudent with his finances, striving to live within his means while providing for his family. He saved aggressively for retirement and spoke to me about buying a retirement home in Florida. He managed to provide a lovely home and a loving environment for his wife and children. His children got an excellent education in a top school district and played college tennis at great schools. He even worked as the head coach in a country club during summers to secure health benefits for himself and his family. He made sure to save and faithfully contribute to his IRA over the years by working hard and being careful with his expenses, managing them closely. I would see him every weekend leading adult clinics, always smiling. I remember him yelling, "Bill, move your feet; you're not on vacation," or "Bill, there are lines on the court for a reason." This balance between professional accomplishment and personal responsibility showcased how a successful life isn't just about earnings but about managing resources wisely and prioritizing what truly matters: family, fulfillment, and community.

Joe's life teaches a powerful lesson: Do what you love and are good at, live within your means, work hard, and give generously of yourself to those around you. By following these principles, he created a life rich in success and full of love.

## HARRY'S STORY

Let me introduce you to Harry. A successful professional in his field, Harry earned a substantial income throughout his career. Unlike Joe, who epitomized the virtues of living within one's means, Harry embraced a lifestyle of opulence and indulgence. He poured his wealth into lavish homes and extravagant vacations, believing the financial wellspring would never run dry. However, Harry's attraction to risky financial ventures and get-rich-quick schemes matched his penchant for luxury. These investments often resulted in substantial losses, yet his spending habits remained unchanged.

As the years progressed, Harry's finances became increasingly unstable. Despite his high earnings, he failed to save or invest wisely for the future. His lifestyle, once the envy of many, became a precarious juggling act, with his fortunes tied up in volatile investments that rarely paid off. The absence of a safety net became painfully apparent as he approached retirement age.

In stark contrast to Joe, who had carefully managed his income and provided security for his family's future, Harry was in a dire situation. He became reliant on his children for support with nothing substantial saved and continuous financial missteps. This placed an unexpected and significant burden on the kids, as they had to care for both Harry and his wife, straining their own resources and affecting the financial security of their own families.

Harry's story is a cautionary tale about the dangers of living beyond one's means, the importance of prudent financial planning, and the necessity of ensuring that living within your means includes, by definition, allocating a portion of your earnings to savings for the future. It highlights that even those with considerable incomes can face financial insecurity if they fail to plan and save responsibly. In contrast, Joe's lifestyle, focused on moderation and careful financial management, ensured that his family remained secure, even though he died so young, and his legacy was a source of inspiration rather than a burden. This juxtaposition underscores a vital life lesson.

> **Living within your means and planning for the future is crucial to a rewarding and sustainable life regardless of income. It's all about making the best financial choices to achieve your goals and honor your values.**

# CONCLUSION

Navigating the forks in the road of retirement planning and investment is a long journey, a marathon in my view, with many opportunities and potential pitfalls. An important takeaway from this book is the concept of the individual as a CEO in managing and overseeing their retirement and financial strategy. Strategy formulation, prudent decision-making, and continual oversight define the successful CEO, and these should compose our overall approach toward managing our own 401(k)s, IRAs, investment portfolios, and careers.

In this book, we've explored how to safeguard our financial futures through leveraging opportunities and navigating potential pitfalls. We've covered how each individual, equipped with knowledge and strategy, can execute their financial affairs with executive skills. We have also learned that this journey does not need to be complicated or require financial genius, but it *is* a marathon, not a sprint. The approach toward your financial future is a continuous, slow progression, guided by a few key principles:

- Keep your eye on your 401(k) and other retirement strategies with the vigilance of a hawk.
- Exercise patience and discipline, taking advantage of time.
- Spend less than you make or, as I have said repeatedly, live within your means.

I also believe in the "KISS" principle. This means *keep it super simple*. Achieving financial security in retirement does not require side gigs or crypto investments. It doesn't involve creative get-rich-quick schemes. It involves understanding your available opportunities and taking steps to optimize your financial position. But planning for a future of peace and satisfaction also requires a holistic approach that is more than crunching numbers. It also means performing at your peak within your workplace, contributing to your organization tirelessly, and always being on the lookout for opportunities where you can add tangible value to your employer, thereby securing your professional and financial footing. Building wealth for your retirement and other purposes is, really, oh so simple, and if you follow the guidance in this book, you will not merely be planning for a future, you will be creating it.

Good luck on your journey! Stay focused. You've got this! Vamos.

# APPENDIX A: SPIVA SCORECARD

The SPIVA Scorecard compares the performance of actively managed US equity funds to the relevant S&P index benchmarks. Note that, over the long term (twenty-year columns), nearly all the actively managed funds underperformed their index.

## SPIVA US SCORECARD YEAR-END 2023

**Report 1a: Percentage of US equity funds underperforming their benchmarks (based on absolute return)**

| SPIVA category | Comparison index | 1-year (%) | 3-year (%) | 5-year (%) | 10-year (%) | 15-year (%) | 20-year (%) |
|---|---|---|---|---|---|---|---|
| All domestic funds | S&P Composite 1500 | 50.29 | 78.69 | 88.01 | 93.14 | 93.95 | 92.14 |
| All large-cap funds | S&P 500 | 51.08 | 74.27 | 86.51 | 91.41 | 93.40 | 94.79 |
| All mid-cap funds | S&P MidCap 400 | 62.60 | 77.97 | 64.78 | 81.51 | 93.22 | 94.04 |
| All small-cap funds | S&P SmallCap 600 | 56.91 | 66.92 | 70.54 | 89.11 | 94.35 | 93.67 |
| All multi-cap funds | S&P Composite 1500 | 50.75 | 81.02 | 87.55 | 93.20 | 94.58 | 93.54 |
| Large-cap growth funds | S&P 500 Growth | 73.85 | 88.94 | 86.09 | 95.89 | 98.15 | 97.65 |
| Large-cap core funds | S&P 500 | 54.30 | 68.27 | 84.01 | 95.91 | 95.69 | 96.38 |
| Large-cap value funds | S&P 500 Value | 58.70 | 39.46 | 69.02 | 84.90 | 79.13 | 86.51 |
| Mid-cap growth funds | S&P MidCap 400 Growth | 91.23 | 78.36 | 38.89 | 65.87 | 91.00 | 91.58 |
| Mid-cap core funds | S&P MidCap 400 | 53.66 | 70.75 | 78.15 | 88.43 | 96.49 | 97.03 |
| Mid-cap value funds | S&P MidCap 400 Value | 72.73 | 81.82 | 83.93 | 95.65 | 93.00 | 92.16 |
| Small-cap growth funds | S&P SmallCap 600 Growth | 79.60 | 75.76 | 58.60 | 84.50 | 95.43 | 96.67 |

| Small-cap core funds | S&P SmallCap 600 | 39.83 | 65.48 | 76.33 | 95.26 | 94.81 | 95.12 |
|---|---|---|---|---|---|---|---|
| Small-cap value funds | S&P SmallCap 600 Value | 40.63 | 43.84 | 80.65 | 90.99 | 91.43 | 92.16 |
| Multi-cap growth funds | S&P Composite 1500 Growth | 56.21 | 85.00 | 84.36 | 89.55 | 96.05 | 91.36 |
| Multi-cap core funds | S&P Composite 1500 | 58.38 | 79.43 | 90.20 | 96.69 | 93.48 | 95.36 |
| Multi-cap value funds | S&P Composite 1500 Value | 58.16 | 58.04 | 86.84 | 91.23 | 90.60 | 88.89 |
| Real estate funds | S&P United States REIT | 87.67 | 58.44 | 61.90 | 74.03 | 87.25 | 87.10 |

*Sources:* S&P Dow Jones Indices. Data as of December 31, 2023.

*Note:* Past performance is no guarantee of future results. The table is provided for illustrative purposes.

# APPENDIX B: GETTING HELP

Besides creating rights for plan participants, ERISA imposes duties on people who use their discretion or judgment in operating your plan. These people are *fiduciaries* and have a legal duty to act prudently and in the interests of plan participants and beneficiaries. Fiduciaries include investment managers, trustees, and plan administrators. If you have questions about your plan, the first place to start is with your SPD. If you need additional assistance, you should contact the plan administrator. The SPD should provide information about how to make contact.

Under ERISA, you can enforce your rights. For example, you can sue in federal court if you request plan documents and don't receive them. Or, if the plan fiduciaries misuse the plan's assets or discriminate against you for exercising your rights, you can get help. Start by referring to your SPD for more information. Then you can seek help from the United States Department of Labor, the Employee Benefits Security Administration, or the Pension Benefit Guaranty Corporation (PBGC), which guarantees certain vested benefits earned under most private defined benefit pension plans. The PBGC does not guarantee defined contribution plans, such as 401(k)s and profit-sharing plans.

You can also contact the IRS for help understanding the rules surrounding tax benefits and consequences.

## FILING A CLAIM FOR BENEFITS

All plan types must follow a reasonable procedure for processing a claim for benefits. Your plan's claim procedures are explained in the SPD. When you become eligible for benefits, you'll complete and

submit a distribution form to the plan administrator. If you don't receive your benefits or believe an error has been made, you can file a
claim. After you file one, keep the following in mind:

- The plan has up to ninety days to decide your claim,
  which can be extended an additional ninety days if you
  are notified.
- You will receive a written notice explaining whether and
  why your claim was denied.
- You will have sixty days to file an appeal in case of a
  denial.
- After your appeal is filed, the plan has up to sixty days to
  decide, which can be extended an additional sixty days if
  you are notified.
- You will receive a written notice explaining whether and
  why your appeal was denied.
- If your claim and appeal are denied, you have the right to
  know why and, without any charge, to obtain any documents relating to the decision.

# APPENDIX C: SAMPLE LINEUP

This information is redacted from the investment offerings of a large company and is a typical lineup. Note that the index fund fees are significantly less expensive than the fees in the actively traded funds. The index funds and fees are shown in gray. You should also note the target date funds and the related fees. As you can see, they are far less than the fees for the other funds.

| Investment Option | | | | | | | |
|---|---|---|---|---|---|---|---|
| | | | | Returns as of Month Ending /20 | | | |
| Asset allocation | Gross/net expense ratio | Inception date | 1 month | 1 year | 3 year | 5 year | 10 years since inception |
| Targeted date retirement fund | .04/.04 | 3/31/2015 | 1.37 | 1.44 | 2.13 | 4.15 | 4.55 |
| Target date fund 2020 | .04/.04 | 3/31/2016 | 1.52 | 1.91 | 2.29 | 4.23 | 5.21 |
| Target date fund 2025 | .04/.04 | 3/31/2015 | 1.84 | 3.44 | 3.63 | 5.04 | 6.19 |
| Target date fund 2030 | .04/.04 | 3/31/2015 | 2.17 | 5.01 | 4.86 | 5.79 | 6.77 |
| Target date fund 2035 | .04/.04 | 3/31/2016 | 2.48 | 6.35 | 5.89 | 6.25 | 7.24 |
| Target date fund 2040 | .04/.04 | 3/31/2015 | 2.72 | 7.37 | 6.72 | 6.57 | 7.56 |
| Target date fund 2045 | .05/.05 | 5/31/201 | 2.98 | 8.25 | 7.84 | 7.10 | 7.85 |
| Target date fund 2050 | .05/.05 | 3/31/2012 | 3.12 | 8.90 | 7.99 | 7.19 | 7.88 |
| Target date fund 2055 | .05/.05 | 3/31/2013 | 3.12 | 8.90 | 7.99 | 7.19 | 7.35 |
| Target date fund 2060 | .05/.05 | 2/28/2018 | 3.12 | 8.90 | 8.00 | 7.20 | 7.26 |
| Target date fund 2065 | .05/.05 | 7/30/2021 | 3.11 | 8.76 | N/A | N/A | -1.98 |
| | | | | | | | |
| **International funds** | | | | | | | |
| Diversified non-US equity fund | .42/.42 | 1/31/2012 | 3.42 | 14.34 | 10.04 | 4.88 | 5.89 |
| Total international stock index | .06/.06 | 1/31/2012 | 3.87 | 12.65 | 7.54 | 4.06 | 5.04 |
| **Specialty** | | | | | | | |
| REIT index | .13/.13 | 1/31/2012 | 2.07 | -9.75 | 5.37 | 4.68 | 6.27 |
| **Mid-cap funds** | | | | | | | |
| Extended market index | .06/.06 | 1/31/2012 | 5.90 | 10.67 | 9.37 | 7.04 | 9.25 |
| **Large-cap funds** | | | | | | | |
| | | | | | | | |
| Diversified US equity fund | .38/.38 | 1/31/2012 | 3.33 | 11.04 | 12.74 | 12.55 | 12.30 |
| Institutional index | .03/.03 | 1/31/2012 | 3.21 | 12.99 | 13.70 | 12.18 | 12.64 |
| **Bond** | | | | | | | |
| US TIPS | .11/.11 | 1/31/2012 | 0.11 | -5.45 | -0.90 | 2.54 | 1.96 |
| Diversified bond fund | .20/.20 | 1/31/2012 | 0.15 | -1.97 | -3.75 | 1.23 | 1.89 |
| Total bond market index | .05/.05 | 1/31/2012 | -0.05 | -3.15 | -4.51 | 0.77 | 1.47 |
| **Money market** | | | | | | | |
| Government fund | .25/.25 | 1/31/2012 | 0.40 | 4.08 | 1.46 | 1.54 | 0.98 |

# APPENDIX D: HOW DOES YOUR 401(k) PLAN STACK UP?

This information presents data based on the PSCA 66th Annual Survey and reflects 401(k) plan experiences for 2022. It is included to help the reader compare their plan features with a broad survey. Key findings are included in certain categories, so trends are flagged. If a particular provision might help you, you can use this to bring it to your plan administrator's attention.

## EMPLOYEE ELIGIBILITY

*Key findings—The percentage of plans allowing hourly part-time employees to participate continues to increase.*

- 93% of US employees are eligible to participate in their plan.
- Almost all plans allow full-time salaried and hourly employees to participate.
- 77% of plans allow part-time salaried and hourly employees to participate, hourly up 3% from the previous year and no change in salaried year over year.
- 29% of companies allow temporary employees to participate.
- 71% of companies all commissioned staff to participate.
- 82% of companies allow employees to begin contributing within three months of hire.
- 72% of companies allow employees to receive matching contributions within three months of hire.

## PARTICIPATION

*Key findings—A significant portion of employees participate, but the percentage of salary contributed is decreasing.*

- 86% of eligible employees made contributions to their plans.
- 7.4% was the average percentage of salary contributed by eligible participants, down over 1% from the previous year.

## ROTH CONTRIBUTIONS

*Key findings—The percentage of plans offering Roth 401(k) contributions continues to increase yet the percentage of participants making these contributions remains low.*

- 89% of plans allow Roth contributions.
- 21% of participants make Roth contributions.

## CATCH-UP CONTRIBUTIONS

*Key findings—Almost all plans allow participants to make catch-up contributions, yet fewer eligible participants made catch than in the previous year.*

- 99.6% of plans allow catch-up contributions.
- 67% of plans match catch-ups.
- 25% of participants made catch-ups, down from 33% from the prior year.

## ROLLOVERS

*Key findings—Almost all plans allow rollovers into the plan from other 401(k) plans, yet less than half of all plans allow rollovers from IRAs.*

- Nearly 100% of plans allow rollovers from other 401(k) plans.
- 47% allow rollovers from IRAs.

## COMPANY CONTRIBUTIONS

*Key findings—Company contributions dropped 0.8% after a record high in 2021 of 5.6%.*

- 4.0% of annual pay was contributed to plans with only matching contributions.
- 4.8% of pay was contributed to plans with both matching and nonmatching contributions.
- 19.2% of plans contribute less than 2% of pay.
- 20.6 of plans contribute between 2–2.9% of pay.

## MOST COMMON MATCHING FORMULAS

*Key findings—3% of pay is the most common formula, although more generous matches are also available in many plans.*

- 22.3% of plans matched $0.50 per $1.00 on the first 6% of pay.
- 9.4% of plans matched $1.00 on the first 3% or less.
- 10.6% of plans matched $1.00 on the first 4%.
- 11.7% of plans matched $1.00 on the first 5%.
- 12.9% of plans matched $1.00 on the first 6%.

## VESTING

*Key findings—Among plans that do not have immediate vesting graduated vesting over several years is the most common arrangement for both matching and nonmatching contributions.*

- 40% of plans immediately vest matching contributions.
- 32.3% of plans immediately vest nonmatching contributions.
- 39.6% of plans vest matching contributions using a graded vesting schedule.
- 42.7% of plans vest nonmatching contributions using a graded vesting schedule.
- 5 and 6 year graded are the most common schedules for matching and nonmatching contributions.
- Employee contributions are always immediately vested.

## INVESTMENT OPTIONS

*Key findings—85.4% of plans offer indexed domestic equity funds.*

- 21 was the average number of funds offered.
- 85.4% offered indexed domestic equity funds.
- 82% offered actively managed domestic equity funds.
- 54.9% offered indexed international equity funds.
- 52.5% offered domestic bond index funds.
- 74.6% offered actively managed bond funds.
- 95% offered target date funds.
- On average, plans offer 2 actively managed domestic bond funds, 1 indexed domestic bond fund, 5.6 actively managed domestic equity funds, 3 indexed domestic equity funds, 1.8 actively managed international equity funds, and 1.2 indexed international equity funds.

## AVERAGE ALLOCATION

*Key findings—Indexed domestic equity funds are a popular option.*

- 29.8% were invested in target date funds.
- 20.3% were invested in indexed domestic equity funds.
- 15.3% were invested in actively managed domestic equity funds.
- 2.9% were invested in indexed international equity funds.
- 3.5% were invested in actively managed international equity funds.
- 3.0% were invested in indexed domestic bond funds.
- 3.4% were invested in actively managed domestic bond funds.

## COMPANY STOCK

*Key findings—Despite 10.7% of plans offering company stock as an option, only 1.1% of total plan assets were invested in this option. This suggests participant's preferences for a more diversified portfolio.*

- 10.7% of plans allowed company stock as an investment option.
- 1.1% of plan assets were invested in company stock.

## AUTOMATIC FEATURES

*Key findings—More plans featured automatic options, including automatic enrollment at rates high enough that employees could receive the full matching contribution.*

## *Automatic Enrollment*

- 63.9% offered an automatic enrollment feature.
- 27.6% used a default rate of 6% of pay.
- 29.2% used a default rate of 3% of pay.
- 63% used a default rate of more than 3% of pay.

## *Automatic Escalation*

- 33.7% automatically increased the default rate for all participants.

## *Automatic Rebalancing*

- 83.4% allowed for automatic rebalancing.


## PLAN LOANS

*Key findings—Most plans have loan features. Almost no plans allow new loans after termination. The repayment of loans after termination feature is much more common, particularly among large organizations.*

- 82.9% permitted participants to borrow against their plan accounts (93.3% of plans with five thousand or more participants).
- 54.6% used the prime rate plus 1% as the loan interest rate, the most common rate.
- 18.6% of participants had a loan outstanding.
- 31.9% allowed participants to repay loans after termination (including 63% of large plans).
- .8% of plans allow participants to take new loans after termination.

## DISTRIBUTIONS

*Key findings—The percentage of participants taking a hardship distribution was low at 1.9%.*

- 91.2% offered hardship distributions.
- 88.6% offered lump sum distributions.
- 55.3% allowed installment distributions.
- 10.3% allowed annuities.
- 84.2% allowed rollovers to another plan.

# APPENDIX E: KEY DOCUMENTS AND INSURANCE

Imagine a future where you and your loved ones are well prepared for unexpected events—when you've safeguarded your assets and ensured peace of mind. Here are some essential documents, beyond the ones we've already discussed for retirement accounts, and insurance options that should be considered as you strive toward that objective.

## DOCUMENTS

Everyone, regardless of age or financial status, should make sure to fill out some key documents to protect loved ones in the event of death or disability. These can often take a few minutes, and some may not require an attorney.

*Advance directive (living will):* This document is like your voice from the beyond. When circumstances prevent you from expressing your wishes, your advance directive steps in. It offers clear instructions to your family and medical professionals about life-saving measures you want or do not want. For instance, it can specify if you prefer not to be placed on a ventilator or receive nutrition through a feeding tube in a life-threatening situation.

*Health care power of attorney (healthcare proxy):* This document allows you to designate *who* will make medical decisions when you can't. This ensures that a trusted person represents your interest during challenging times.

*Revocable living trust:* Think trusts are only for the wealthy? Think again! This flexible trust lets you control your finances while you're alive and grants someone you choose the power to manage them if needed. Plus, it bypasses the expensive and time-consuming *probate* process when you die, saving money and time. (Probate is the process of getting a deceased person's will approved by a court and then settling the estate.)

*Last will and testament:* No matter your financial status, a will is necessary. It outlines how your assets and wealth should be distributed after your passing and even allows you to designate a guardian for your children. Without a will, state laws will determine the fate of your assets.

*Durable financial power of attorney:* Imagine you're temporarily incapacitated, but bills still need to be paid. With this document, a trusted individual can manage your finances or liaise with companies on your behalf, ensuring your financial matters are handled smoothly.

## INSURANCE

Insurance is designed to protect you from financial loss when bad things happen. Multiple types of insurance are available, and policies vary based on all kinds of factors, including premiums and deductibles as well as the level of risk that the insurance underwriter believes you present. Remember to shop around and compare quotes to find the best rates. Bundling insurance policies can also help you save on costs. Prepare today to secure your family's tomorrow!

*Life insurance:* Life insurance provides financial security for your family if you pass away. It pays a sum to your beneficiaries, helping cover lost income because you are no longer here to work or to help them repay debts you left behind. *Term* life insurance is popular and affordable, providing coverage for a particular number of years, such as ten or twenty. If the insured dies during the term, the death benefit is paid. If death occurs outside the term, no death benefit is paid. Other life insurance options include *whole* and *universal* life.

*Disability insurance:* Did you know a twenty-year-old worker has a one in four chance of becoming disabled before retirement?[1] This insurance covers a portion of your income if you can't work due to illness or injury. There are short-term and long-term coverage options with varying payout percentages and conditions, and many employers offer this as part of their benefit package.

*Health insurance:* Medical bills can quickly drain your savings. Health insurance may come with copays and deductibles, but it helps offset the high costs of medical treatments. If you're not covered through your job, you can explore options through online marketplaces, keeping in mind that there are special enrollment periods that restrict when you can enroll or make changes.

*Auto insurance:* If you're a driver, you're likely required by law to have auto insurance. The minimum coverage varies by state, but it's essential for protecting yourself and others on the road. Consider additional coverage like collision and comprehensive to safeguard your vehicle.

*Homeowner's or renter's insurance:* Homeowner's insurance is often mandatory for those with mortgages, but it's a wise investment regardless. It protects your home and possessions from loss stemming from fire or other unforeseen disasters. Renters should consider renter's insurance for liability and personal property protection. Also, consider an umbrella insurance policy. This insurance provides much larger limits for personal liability exposure than provided in your auto or homeowner's policies.

# GLOSSARY

**401(k) plan**—A defined contribution plan where an employee can make contributions from their paycheck, usually before tax (except for Roth contributions), into a 401(k) account. The employee often chooses the investments based on options provided under the plan. In some plans, the employer matches the employee's contributions to a certain percentage. Withdrawals from the plan are taxed and subject to various restrictions.

**account balance**—The total amount of money (or value of other assets) in a financial account, such as a 401(k) account, at any given date.

**actively managed funds**—Mutual funds managed by financial experts who make strategic decisions to try to outperform the market based on research and analysis.

**annual return**—The yearly percentage gain or loss on an investment, including interest, dividends, and capital gains.

**annuity**—A financial product that provides a series of payments at regular intervals. If the annuity, often used for retirement income, is payable over the individual's life, it is referred to as a *life annuity*. If it is payable over two lives, such as for a husband and wife, it is referred to as a joint and survivor annuity.

**asset allocation**—The strategy of dividing assets among different classes, such as equity, fixed income, and others, to manage risk.

**automatic enrollment**—A plan feature where employers automatically deduct a certain percentage from each eligible employee's paycheck and deposit it into their 401(k) account unless they opt out.

**automatic escalation**—A plan feature that automatically increases an employee's 401(k) contribution percentages over time. Employees can usually opt out of this feature.

**bond**—A financial instrument issued by a corporation or governmental entity to raise money for a set period with a promise to repay those borrowed funds upon maturity. Bond terms usually include a set interest rate.

**bond index fund**—A broadly diversified mix of bonds in a mutual fund designed to track the performance of a specific bond index, like the Bloomberg US Aggregate Bond Index.

**catch-up contributions**—The additional amounts that individuals aged fifty or older can contribute to their 401(k)s beyond the normal limit. This helps them prepare for retirement when they can most afford it.

**company stock (also known as employer securities)**—Shares of the company representing ownership that may be offered to employees as part of their 401(k) plan.

**compounding**—The process by which the earnings on an investment generate additional earnings, leading to exponential growth over time. The earnings often exceed the original principal.

**contingent beneficiary**—A person designated by the account owner to receive all or a portion of their benefits if the primary beneficiary dies.

**defined benefit plans (also known as pension plans)**—A traditional pension plan that promises the participant a specified monthly benefit at retirement. Often, the benefit is based on factors such as the participant's salary, age, and the number of years they worked for the employer.

**defined contribution plan**—A retirement plan into which the employee, the employer, or both can contribute to the employee's account under the plan. The amount in the account at distribution includes the contributions and investment gains or losses minus any investment and administrative fees. Tax consequences vary depending on the type of contribution—traditional 401(k), Roth 401(k), or profit-sharing plan.

**designated beneficiary**—The individual named by an account owner to receive assets from 401(k), IRA, other retirement plans, financial accounts, or insurance policies after the account owner's death. The plan, insurance company, or financial institution provides a form for this purpose.

**diversification of investments**—Spreading investments across different companies and industries to reduce risk.

**dividend**—Payment by a company to its stockholders, generally from profits.

**domestic bond fund**—A mutual fund that invests in bonds issued by corporations and government entities within the United States.

**Dow Jones Industrial Average (DJIA)**—An index that measures the stock performance of thirty large publicly owned companies in the United States. It is often used as a barometer for the performance of the US stock market.

**Dow Jones US Total Stock Market Index**—An index that measures the performance of all US equity securities. It is often used as a barometer for the performance of the US stock market.

**Employee Retirement Income Security Act of 1974 (ERISA)**—The federal law that sets protection standards for individuals in most voluntarily established, private-sector retirement plans.

**equity**—See **stocks**.

**equity indexed international fund**—A mutual fund that invests in the stock of companies outside the United States and tracks or mirrors the performance of a particular index, such as the FTSE Global All Cap ex US Index.

**fiduciary**—Anyone who exercises discretionary authority or control over the management or administration of a retirement plan or its assets or who gives investment advice for a fee or other compensation concerning the plan's assets. Fiduciaries have a duty under ERISA to act in the sole interests of participants and beneficiaries.

**hardship withdrawal**—A withdrawal from a retirement plan because of an immediate and heavy financial need, usually limited to the amount necessary to satisfy that need.

**index funds**—Mutual funds created to match the returns of an index, such as the S&P 500.

**individual retirement account (IRA)**—A tax-advantaged account set up with a financial institution, such as a bank or mutual fund company, that individuals use to save for retirement. Under federal law, individuals can set aside personal savings up to specified limits and sometimes take a tax deduction for the contributions. The investments grow either tax-free, in the case of a Roth IRA, or tax-deferred, in the case of a traditional IRA.

**in-service withdrawals**—Distributions that an employee can make from a retirement plan under certain conditions, such as on account of hardship or upon reaching age fifty-nine and a half.

**international fund**—A mutual fund that invests in the stock of companies outside the United States.

**large-cap equity**—Companies with a high market value (known as *market capitalization*), typically over $10 billion.

**market capitalization**—The total market value of a company's out-standing shares of stock, which is equal to its current stock price times the number of outstanding shares.

**match or matching contribution**—The employer's contribution to a 401(k) plan that matches the employee's own contributions up to a limit, often stated as a percentage of compensation.

**mid-cap equity**—Companies with a value (also known as market cap-italization), typically between $2 billion and $10 billion.

**modified adjusted gross income (MAGI)**—Adjusted gross income, as reported on Form 1040, plus a few items, such as student loan in-terest deduction, excluded savings bond interest, foreign-earned income exclusion, housing exclusion, foreign housing deduction, ex-cluded employer-provided adoption benefits, Social Security benefits excluded from taxable income, and passive losses. For Roth purposes, MAGI also includes Roth conversion amounts.

**mutual fund**—A professionally managed portfolio of stocks, bonds, real estate, and other assets funded by many investors.

**Nasdaq**—A global electronic stock exchange or marketplace for buy-ing and selling securities and a benchmark index for US technology stocks.

**participant**—An eligible employee covered by a retirement plan.

**per stirpes**—A method of distributing property in the event of a 401(k) or IRA owner's death. Under this method, if a beneficiary predeceases the owner, their share of the owner's account is distributed to the ben-eficiary's descendants.

**plan administrator**—The person or company identified in the plan document responsible for managing the plan. It could be the employer, a committee of employees, a company executive, or someone from outside the company hired for that purpose.

**plan document**—A written instrument under which the plan is established and operated. It contains all the key features, benefits, and obligations.

**profit-sharing plan**—A defined contribution plan under which the employer may determine, annually, how much will be contributed (out of profits or otherwise) to the employees. A profit-sharing plan may include a 401(k) feature.

**rebalancing investments**—The process of changing the percentage of an investment over a set frequency (e.g., quarterly) in an account or portfolio to maintain a preferred asset allocation.

**required minimum distribution (RMD)**—The minimum amount that must be withdrawn annually from a retirement plan or IRA starting at age seventy-three (age seventy-five beginning in 2033). Account owners in employer plans, such as a 401(k), can delay taking their RMDs until they retire after the specified age. Roth accounts generally do not require RMDs during the life of the owner. RMDs are required on the death of an owner in an IRA or 401(k).

**retirement calculator**—A tool that helps estimate the amount needed for retirement based on current savings, retirement age, life expectancy, and other factors. It can also help with other decision-making, like whether to make a Roth or traditional contribution.

**rollover**—The transfer of retirement savings by a participant from a retirement account or IRA to a new plan or IRA without triggering taxes or penalties.

**Roth account**—A retirement account where contributions are made with after-tax dollars, and withdrawals are generally tax-free. Roth accounts may be available as a 401(k) or IRA.

**Roth contribution**—A contribution to a Roth IRA or 401(k) made with after-tax dollars.

**Roth conversion**—The transfer of funds from a traditional IRA or 401(k) to a Roth IRA or 401(k), which requires taxes to be paid on the converted amount. Later withdrawals are generally tax-free.

**S&P 500 index**—An index tracking the stock performance of five hundred large companies listed on US stock exchanges that seeks to benchmark the entire US stock market.

**service crediting**—The process by which a participant's service is calculated for vesting, eligibility, and benefit accrual.

**small-cap equity**—Companies with a value (known as *market capitalization*), typically between $250 million and $2 billion.

**Social Security**—A federal program providing financial benefits to retirees and the disabled.

**stocks (also known as equity)**—A financial security that represents ownership of a fraction of a corporation, providing the shareholder a right to a portion of the company's assets and earnings based on their level of stock ownership.

**summary plan description (SPD)**—A document provided by the plan administrator that includes a plain language description of important features of the plan, including a definition of compensation, eligibility requirements, service crediting, investment alternatives, and so on.

**tax deduction**—An expense that can be subtracted from taxable income, decreasing the income subject to income tax.

**total stock market funds**—Mutual funds that aim to duplicate the performance of an entire stock market, like the US stock market.

**traditional contribution**—Contributions to a traditional 401(k) or IRA with pre-tax dollars that decrease taxable income.

**true-up matching contribution**—An additional contribution made by an employer under certain circumstances to ensure that the total annual match is made to participants who fail to receive their match for technical reasons before the end of the year.

**trustee**—The individual or entity responsible for prudently managing the 401(k) assets in the best interest of participants and beneficiaries.

**vesting schedule**—The period over which employees obtain full and nonforfeitable ownership of employer-provided retirement benefits, such as matching contributions.

**yield**—The rate of return on an investment displayed as a percentage. It is calculated by dividing the annual dividend or interest by the investment cost. In the case of bonds, the interest is divided by the purchase price. In the case of stocks, the dividend per share is divided by the stock price per share.

# NOTES

## INTRODUCTION

1    Diane Oakley, Jennifer Brown, and Joelle Saad-Lassler, "Retirement in America: Out of Reach for Working Americans?," National Institute on Retirement Security (NIRS), September 2018, https://www.nirsonline.org/reports/retirement-in-america-out-of-reach-for-most-americans/.

2    Oakley et al., "Retirement in America."

3    Dan Doonan and Kelly Kenneally, "Retirement Insecurity 2024: Americans' Views of Retirement," National Institute on Retirement Security (NIRS), February 2024, https://www.nirsonline.org/reports/retirementinsecurity2024/.

4    Yin Yimeng, Anqi Chen, and Alicia Munnell, "The National Retirement Risk Index: Version 2.0," Center for Retirement Research at Boston College, May 9, 2023, https://crr.bc.edu/the-national-retirement-risk-index-version-2-0/.

## CHAPTER 2

1    "S&P 500 Return Calculator, with Dividend Reinvestment," DQYDJ, August 16, 2024, https://dqydj.com/sp-500-return-calculator/.

2    "S&P 500 Index—90 Year Historical Chart," Macrotrends, 2024, https://www.macrotrends.net/2324/sp-500-historical-chart-data.

3    "S&P 500 Return Calculator."

4    "Time, Not Timing, Is What Matters," Capital Group American Funds, accessed October 26, 2024, https://www.capitalgroup.com/individual/planning/investing-fundamentals/time-not-timing-is-what-matters.html.

5    "S&P 500 Return Calculator."

6    "Generation Returns," Crestmont Research, 2024, https://www.crestmontresearch.com/docs/Stock-20-Yr-Returns.pdf.

7    "Dow Jones Industrial Average: From 1970 through 1979," 1728 Software Systems, 2024, https://www.1728.org/djia1970.htm.

8    "Dow Jones Industrial Average Return Calculator, Dividends

Reinvested," DQYDJ, August 16, 2024, accessed May 12, 2024, https://dqydj.com/dow-jones-return-calculator/.

9    Jill Bebar, "Record Century: Dow, Nasdaq, S&P Cap Phenomenal Year, Decade at All-time Highs," CNN Money, December 21, 1999, accessed May 12, 2024, https://money.cnn.com/1999/12/31/markets/markets _newyork/.

10   Ben Rooney, "Are Investors Joining Rally Too Late?," CNN Business, October 31, 2013, accessed May 12, 2024, https://money.cnn.com /2013/10/31/investing/stocks-inflow/index.html.

11   Brian Duignan, "Dot-Com Bubble," Encyclopedia Britannica, September 19, 2024, https://www.britannica.com/money/dot-com -bubble.

12   *Monthly Mutual Fund Report—2002 Review: Statistics for December 2002–January 2003*, Federal Reserve Bank of Boston, 2003.

13   *Monthly Mutual Fund Report—2002 Review.*

14   Amy Arnott, "How to Use International Stocks in Your Portfolio," Morningstar, September 16, 2024, https://www.morningstar.com /portfolios/how-use-international-stocks-your-portfolio.

15   Arnott, "How to Use International Stocks."

16   Ian Kresnak, "Making the Case for International Equity Allocations," Vanguard, May 5, 2023, https://corporate.vanguard.com/content /corporatesite/us/en/corp/articles/making-case-international-equity -allocations.html.

17   Amy Arnott, "Revisiting the Case for International," Morningstar, November 14, 2019, https://www.morningstar.com/stocks/revisiting -case-international.

18   John Christy, "Investing in International Stock Funds," The Balance, January 30, 2022, https://www.thebalancemoney.com/how-much -international-exposure-should-you-have-1979001.

19   Anu R. Ganti et al., *SPIVA U.S. Year-End 2023*, S&P Global, March 6, 2024, https://www.spglobal.com/spdji/en/documents/spiva/spiva-us -year-end-2023.pdf?gclid=undefined.

20   Ganti et al., *SPIVA U.S. Year-End 2023.*

21   Plan Sponsor Council of America, *PSCA's 65th Annual Survey of Profit Sharing and 401(k) Plans*, 2022.

22   Zachary Evens and Bryan Armour, "The 2023 US Fund Fee Study: Morningstar Manager Research," Morningstar, July 2024, https://assets.contentstack.io/v3/assets/blt4eb669caa7dc65b2 /blt7b54038c40308f13/668c241bcf6f65d1556e706b/2023_US_Fund _Fee_Study.pdf.

23   Jeff Sommer, "A Mutual Fund Master, Too Worried to Rest," *New*

*York Times*, August 11, 2012, https://www.nytimes.com/2012/08/12 /business/john-bogle-vanguards-founder-is-too-worried-to-rest.html.

## CHAPTER 3

1    Chris Mamula, "The One Thing That Determines Financial Success or Failure," Can I Retire Yet?, November 20, 2023, https://www .caniretireyet.com/living-below-your-means/.

2    "How Much Will You Spend in Retirement?," Fidelity, November 14, 2023, https://www.fidelity.com/viewpoints/retirement/spending-in -retirement.

3    "4 Rules for Retirement Savings: Consider These 4 Guidelines to Help You on Your Retirement Journey," Fidelity, February 28, 2024, https://www.fidelity.com/viewpoints/retirement/retirement-guidelines.

4    "4 Rules for Retirement Savings."

5    "How Much Do I Need to Retire?: Fidelity's Guideline: Save 10x Your Income by Age 67," Fidelity, April 24, 2024, https://www.fidelity.com /viewpoints/retirement/how-much-do-i-need-to-retire.

6    Phillip L. Cooley, Carl M. Hubbard, and Daniel T. Walz, "Retirement Savings: Choosing a Withdrawal Rate That Is Sustainable," American Association of Individual Investors Journal, February 1988, https://www .aaii.com/files/pdf/6794_retirement-savings-choosing-a-withdrawal -rate-that-is-sustainable.pdf.

7    Chris Mamula and Darrow Kirkpatrick, "Can I Retire Yet?," Can I Retire Yet?, https://www.canIretireyet.com.

8    Jennifer Brozic, "Average Car Payment in 2024," Experian, October 28, 2024, https://www.experian.com/blogs/ask-experian/average-car -payment/.

9    "Car Payment Calculator," Carvana, accessed December 15, 2024, https://www.carvana.com/auto-loan-calculator.

10   Felix Richter, "U.S. Consumer Debt Climbs to $17.3 Trillion," *Statista Daily Data*, November 9, 2023, https://www.statista.com/chart/19955 /household-debt-balance-in-the-united-states/.

11   Richter, "U.S. Consumer Debt Climbs."

12   "Credit Card Calculator," Calculator.net, 2010, accessed October 27, 2024, https://www.calculator.net/credit-card-calculator.html.

13   Hearst Autos Research, "What Is Car Depreciation?," *Car and Driver*, 2024, https://www.caranddriver.com/research/a31481267/car -depreciation/.

## CHAPTER 4

1    PSCA's Research Committee, *66th Annual Survey of Profit Sharing and 401(k) Plans* (Arlington, VA: Plan Sponsor Council of America (PSCA), 2023).

## CHAPTER 5

1    PSCA's Research Committee, *66th Annual Survey of Profit Sharing and 401(k) Plans* (Arlington, VA: PSCA, 2023).

2    Market cap is calculated by multiplying the total number of company shares outstanding by the current stock price. The definitions are as follows:
    *Large-cap:* Market cap of $10 billion or more.
    *Mid-cap:* Market cap between $2 billion and $10 billion.
    *Small-cap:* Market cap between $250 million and $2 billion.
    *Micro-cap:* Market cap less than $250 million.
    "Market Cap Explained," FINRA, September 30, 2022, https://www.finra.org/investors/insights/market-cap.

3    Kent Thune, "Total Stock Market Index vs. S&P 500 Index," The Balance, July 10, 2024, https://www.thebalancemoney.com/total-stock-market-vs-sandp-500-2466403.

4    John Rekenthaler, "The Best Total U.S. Stock Market Funds," Morningstar, April 11, 2022, https://www.morningstar.com/columns/rekenthaler-report/best-total-us-stock-market-funds.

5    Zachary Evens and Bryan Armour, "The 2023 US Fund Fee Study: Morningstar Manager Research," Morningstar, 2024, https://assets.contentstack.io/v3/assets/blt4eb669caa7dc65b2/blt7b54038c4030 8f13/668c241bcf6f65d1556e706b/2023_US_Fund_Fee_Study.pdf.

6    Evens and Armour, "2023 US Fund Fee Study."

7    Ganti et al., *SPIVA U.S. Year-End 2023.*

8    Ganti et al., *SPIVA U.S. Year-End 2023.*

9    *66th Annual Survey of Profit Sharing and 401(k) Plans.*

10   Ganti et al., *SPIVA U.S. Year-End 2023.*

11   Amy C. Arnott, "How Long Will It Take The Market to Recover?" Morningstar, January 30, 2023, https://www.morningstar.com/portfolios/how-long-will-it-take-market-recover.

12   *66th Annual Survey of Profit Sharing and 401(k) Plans.*

# CHAPTER 6

1    PSCA's Research Committee, *66th Annual Survey of Profit Sharing and 401(k) Plans* (Arlington, VA: PSCA, 2023).
2    I changed the interest rate assumption to help reinforce that the returns are not guaranteed and fluctuate.

# CHAPTER 7

1    PSCA's Research Committee, *66th Annual Survey of Profit Sharing and 401(k) Plans* (Arlington, VA: PSCA, 2023).

# CHAPTER 8

1    PSCA's Research Committee, *66th Annual Survey of Profit Sharing and 401(k) Plans* (Arlington, VA: PSCA, 2023).
2    *66th Annual Survey of Profit Sharing and 401(k) Plans.*

# CHAPTER 9

1    Employee Benefits Security Administration (EBSA), *Fact Sheet: Final Rule to Improve Transparency of Fees and Expenses to Workers in 401(k)-Type Retirement Plans*, US Department of Labor, February 2012, https://www.dol.gov/sites/dolgov/files/EBSA/about-ebsa/our-activities /resource-center/fact-sheets/dol-transparent-401k-fees-fact-sheet.pdf.

# CHAPTER 10

1    Fiona Greig, Kelly Hahn, and Fu Tan, *Job Transitions Slow Retirement Savings*, Vanguard, September 2024, https://digital-assets.vanguard .com/corp/research/pdf/job_transitions_slow_retirement_savings.pdf.
2    Anne Tergesen, "The 401(k) Rollover Mistake That Costs Retirement Savers Billions," *Wall Street Journal*, July 22, 2024, https://www .wsj.com/personal-finance/retirement/the-401-k-rollover-mistake -that-costs-retirement-savers-billions-c7a19dfa; Andy Reed et al., *Improving Retirement Outcomes by Default: The Case for an IRA QDIA*, Vanguard, July 2024, https://digital-assets.vanguard.com/corp/public -policy/policy-research/improving_retirement_outcomes_by_default _the_case_for_an_ira_qdia.pdf.

3       Jean Folger, "Which Retirement Funds Are Protected From Creditors?,"
        Investopedia, April 22, 2024, https://www.investopedia.com/articles
        /personal-finance/040716/which-retirement-funds-are-protected
        -creditors.asp.
4       Folger, "Which Retirement Funds Are Protected?"
5       "Rollovers of Retirement Plan and IRA Distributions," IRS, August
        20, 2024, https://www.irs.gov/retirement-plans/plan-participant-
        employee/rollovers-of-retirement-plan-and-ira-distributions; "IRS
        Announcement 2014-32," IRS, https://www.irs.gov/irb/2014-48
        _IRB#ANN-2014-32; "IRS Announcement 2014-15," IRS, https://www
        .irs.gov/irb/2014-16_IRB#ANN-2014-15.

## CHAPTER 11

1       Christine Benz, "Is It Ever a Good Idea to Hold Company Stock in a
        401(k)?," Morningstar, September 4, 2020, https://www.morningstar
        .com/retirement/is-it-ever-good-idea-hold-company-stock-401k.

## CHAPTER 12

1       "Prime Rate History," FedPrimeRate.com, November 7, 2014, https://
        www.fedprimerate.com/wall_street_journal_prime_rate_history.htm.
2       "6 Tips to Navigate Volatile Markets," Fidelity, October 25, 2024,
        https://www.fidelity.com/viewpoints/investing-ideas/six-tips.
3       Denny Ceizyk, "What Is the Average Personal Loan Interest Rate?,"
        Bankrate, October 16, 2024, https://www.bankrate.com/loans/personal
        -loans/average-personal-loan-rates/.
4       Steve Garmhausen, "How Much Should I Have in Savings?," Buy Side
        from WSJ, Wall Street Journal, August 23, 2024, https://www.wsj.com
        /buyside/personal-finance/banking/how-much-should-i-have-in
        -savings.

## CHAPTER 13

1       Ashlea Ebeling, "Your Will Alone Won't Guarantee Your Money Goes
        to Your Heirs," *Wall Street Journal*, September 30, 2023, https://www
        .wsj.com/personal-finance/estate-planning-will-money-family-heirs
        -8f2eb6e8.
2       Ebeling, "Your Will Alone Won't Guarantee."
3       Ebeling, "Your Will Alone Won't Guarantee."

## CHAPTER 14

1 "Economic News Release: Table 1. Retirement Benefits: Access, Participation, and Take-Up Rates," US Bureau of Labor Statistics, March 2024, https://www.bls.gov/news.release/ebs2.t01.htm.
2 Anqi Chen and Alicia H. Munnell, "Who Contributes to Individual Retirement Accounts?," Center for Retirement Research, April 2017, https://crr.bc.edu/wp-content/uploads/2017/04/IB_17-8.pdf.
3 Internal Revenue Code § 408(o)(2).
4 Ashlea Ebeling, "The Secret to Saving for Retirement: Start Before You're 20," *Wall Street Journal*, September 23, 2023, https://www.wsj.com/personal-finance/retirement/these-teens-opened-roth-iras-before-they-could-even-vote-ad2b2a9d.
5 Ebeling, "Secret to Saving for Retirement."
6 "IRA Contribution Limits for 2023 and 2024," Fidelity, March 4, 2024, https://www.fidelity.com/learning-center/smart-money/ira-contribution-limits.
7 "Roth IRA Contribution Limits for 2023 and 2024," Fidelity, March 4, 2024, https://www.fidelity.com/learning-center/smart-money/roth-ira-contribution-limits.

## CHAPTER 15

1 "401(k) Plan Fix-It Guide—Eligible Employees Weren't Given the Opportunity to Make an Elective Deferral Election (Excluding Eligible Employees)," IRS, August 19, 2024, https://www.irs.gov/retirement-plans/401k-plan-fix-it-guide-eligible-employees-werent-given-the-opportunity-to-make-an-elective-deferral-election-excluding-eligible-employees.
2 "401(k) Plan Fix-It Guide—Eligible Employees."

## CHAPTER 16

1 "401(k) Plan Fix-It Guide—You Didn't Use the Plan Definition of Compensation Correctly for All Deferrals and Allocations," IRS, August 26, 2024, https://www.irs.gov/retirement-plans/401k-plan-fix-it-guide-you-didnt-use-the-plan-definition-of-compensation-correctly-for-all-deferrals-and-allocations.
2 "401(k) Plan Fix-It Guide—You Didn't Use the Plan Definition."
3 "401(k) Plan Fix-It Guide—You Didn't Use the Plan Definition."

## CHAPTER 17

1   "Fixing Common Plan Mistakes—Failure to Timely Start Minimum Distributions," IRS, August 19, 2024, https://www.irs.gov/retirement -plans/plan-sponsor/fixing-common-plan-mistakes-failure-to-timely -start-minimum-distributions.

2   "IRS Notice 2024-35: Certain Required Minimum Distributions for 2024," IRS, April 16, 2024, https://www.irs.gov/pub/irs-drop/n-24-35 .pdf; "Notice 2023-54: Transition Relief and Guidance Relating to Certain Required Minimum Distributions," IRS, 2023, https://www.irs .gov/pub/irs-drop/n-23-54.pdf.

## CHAPTER 18

1   Rakesh Kochhar, Kim Parker, and Ruth Igielnik, "Majority of U.S. Workers Changing Jobs Are Seeing Real Wage Gains," Pew Research Center, July 28, 2022, https://www.pewresearch.org/social -trends/2022/07/28/majority-of-u-s-workers-changing-jobs-are-seeing -real-wage-gains/.

2   "29 CFR 2530.200b-1—Computation Periods," Code of Federal Regulations, accessed April 29, 2024, https://www.ecfr.gov/current /title-29/subtitle-B/chapter-XXV/subchapter-D/part-2530/subpart-A /section-2530.200b-1.

## CHAPTER 19

1   "Fixing Common Mistakes—Correcting a Roth Contribution Failure," IRS, August 19, 2024, https://www.irs.gov/retirement-plans/fixing -common-mistakes-correcting-a-roth-contribution-failure.

2   "Fixing Common Mistakes."

3   PSCA's Research Committee, *66th Annual Survey of Profit Sharing and 401(k) Plans* (Arlington, VA: PSCA, 2023).

## CHAPTER 22

1   "29 CFR 2530.203-3—Suspension of Pension Benefits Upon Employment," Code of Federal Regulations, accessed April 29, 2024, https://www.ecfr.gov/current/title-29/subtitle-B/chapter-XXV /subchapter-D/part-2530/subpart-B/section-2530.203-3.

2   Treasury Regulation § 1.411(c)-1(f)(1), Internal Revenue Code § 411(c)(3).

## CHAPTER 23

1    J. L. Collins, *Pathfinders: Extraordinary Stories of People Like You on the Quest for Financial Independence—and How to Join Them* (Harrman House, 2023).

2    Lisa Mad Money Monster, "Why We Ditched the FIRE Movement and Couldn't Be Happier," MarketWatch, October 1, 2019, https://www .marketwatch.com/story/why-we-ditched-the-fire-movement-and -couldnt-be-happier-2019-09-30.

## APPENDIX E

1    "Fact Sheet: Social Security," Social Security Administration, 2024, https://www.ssa.gov/news/press/factsheets/basicfact-alt.pdf.

# ABOUT THE AUTHOR

William A. Bader, JD, CPA, is a retired attorney and consultant with extensive experience in retirement planning and compliance. During his over twenty-five-year career at Mercer, one of the world's largest leading global retirement and human resources consulting firms, Bader held leadership roles, including serving as a worldwide partner. At Mercer, he helped some of the world's largest organizations manage their 401(k) and other retirement plans, conducted fiduciary training for plan fiduciaries, including plan committee members, and reviewed the administration of hundreds of 401(k) plans to ensure compliance and efficiency. Before joining Mercer, he practiced pension, 401(k), and tax law at several law firms, including Fried Frank. Bader is a graduate of the University of Pennsylvania's Wharton School and Hofstra Law School.